EARLY PRAISE FOR RETHINK, REA

Paula Skaper shows leaders how to turn chaos into clarity, confidence, and control. This book is direct, practical, and built for anyone serious about growth in uncertain times.
David Newman, Author of Do It! Selling and Market Eminence

Rethink, Realign, Reinvent is the kind of book leaders need right now. Paula has lived it, led through it, and it shows. She gets to the truth of what it takes to lead when everything around you is shifting.
Angie Whitfield, CEO, Burnaby Board of Trade

This isn't just a book about surviving chaos, it's about how to win because of it. More than theory, it's a battle-tested playbook for entrepreneurial leadership.
Cathy Kuzel, CEO & founder, When Women Talk

Paula Skaper doesn't pretend chaos can be avoided. She shows how to use it as fuel for growth. Rethink, Realign, Reinvent is a practical guide every leader navigating uncertainty, which means every leader ever, should keep within reach.
Jeff Rogers, Award-Winning Speaker
Wall Street Journal and USA Today Best Selling Author

Paula is a master at aligning vision and execution. There's no one better to provide an unvarnished guidebook to leading through chaos. Her approach is refreshingly frank and actionable.
Pete Steege, Author of Radical Clarity
Founder, B2B Clarity

What I love about Paula's work is how human it is, sharp, clear, and deeply practical. This is the kind of book that belongs on your desk, not your shelf, because it is a roadmap leaders can actually use to realign, reinvent, and grow stronger in the chaos.

Susan Goebel, CEO & Founder, Scaling Management Consulting Group

I've had the joy of collaborating with Paula. She brings sharp insight, a grounded approach, and deep care for people. Her clarity when everything feels uncertain helps leaders rethink assumptions without losing what matters most. She offers practical tools and fresh perspective for building what's next with courage and purpose.

Deborah Reuben, CLFP
CEO & Founder, TomorrowZone

I know Paula, and this book reflects the same authentic, pragmatic, no-nonsense insight I've always valued from her. Drawing on lived experiences and work with countless clients across various industries, Rethink, Realign, Reinvent strips away the noise and shows business leaders how to turn chaos into confidence and disruption into strength.

Cory Redekop
CEO, Greater Langley Chamber of Commerce

Rethink, Realign, Reinvent is what happens when sharp strategy meets human-centered leadership. Paula doesn't just challenge hustle culture, she replaces it with something more practical and sustainable.

Erika Woldman Hecht
Author of The Leader Effect
CEO, Market Ascent

This book is about more than surviving chaos. It's about transforming crisis into an advantage. Paula gives leaders the clarity and focus to find opportunities where others only see problems.

Tim Fitzpatrick
Founder, Rialto Marketing

Thanks to working with Paula on strategy for my *Working On Purpose* approach to career planning, we are already established throughout Alberta and Nunavut, and making inroads to several other provinces. I regularly use the tools from her Growth Architecture Framework when selling my program and approach. With this book I feel like I have her 'Paula brain' at my fingertips 24-7.

Steve Miller, Creator - Working On Purpose

It's a jungle out there and although there is no shortage of 'how to books' I haven't seen anything else like this. A practical field-guide for anyone trying to navigate strategy, work a plan and work thoughtfully in this chaotic world, it is clear and deeply insightful, intertwining actionable steps that can be immediately put into practice.

Lynda Barr
General Manager, Dianes Lingerie

Too many leaders chase the next tactic while ignoring the foundation. Paula flips that script. This book is a straight-shooting guide for leaders who want to realign around what matters and position themselves to thrive when others retreat.

Jeff Pugel
Founder, Ignition LLC

I help CEOs communicate, and every conversation is about change—how to anticipate it, how to drive it, and how to respond to it. At last, here's a resource that makes it easier to get ahead of change. In this book, Paula Skaper delivers a clear, practical framework for leaders navigating uncertainty. There's no sugar-coating and no jargon, just straight talk about what's at stake and what it really takes to emerge stronger and more resilient. Even if you only read the section on the eight mistakes that hinder growth, you'll walk away with more than many business books. And that's just the beginning of the wisdom you'll find in these pages.

Pete Weissman,

CEO Communications Advisor

"I've known Paula for years, and let me tell you—this book is peak Paula. Bold, insightful, and just the right amount of provocative. Rethink, Realign, Reinvent doesn't just offer a survival strategy for chaotic times—it hands you the blueprint to grow stronger in the middle of the storm. Paula has a knack for stripping away fluff and delivering the kind of tough-love clarity every leader needs. You won't get coddled, but you'll come away smarter, sharper, and ready to do actually something with your strategy."

—Aaron Cruikshank, President, CTRS Market Intelligence

"Paula is experienced and to the point. This book helps business owners find calm in the chaos which is business. Rethink, Realign, Reinvent is what every business needs as a foundation to build something truly resilient."

Behdad Jamshidi, Founder, CJAM - The Marketing Connector

RETHINK

REALIGN

REINVENT

How Bold Leaders Navigate Chaos to Build a Business that is Crisis-Proof and Future-Ready

PAULA SKAPER

33Dolphins

Cataloguing in publication information is available from Library and Archives Canada.

ISBN 978-1-0698515-0-5 (Paperback)

ISBN 978-1-0698515-2-9 (eBook)

ISBN 978-1-0698515-3-6 (audiobook)

ISBN 978-1-0698515-1-2 (hardcover)

Published by:

33Dolphins Press

33dolphins.com

Cover art & interior design by Victoria Ajadi

PaulaSkaper.com

For Dad.

You believed I could do anything I put my mind to, and you

made me believe it too. I wish I could have seen your smile when

I put this book in your hands.

BEFORE YOU START

My journey into entrepreneurship is probably not that different from yours. An expert in your field, master of your craft, you have chosen to pursue a bigger dream. Your courage is the spirit that defines us. It is the spark that inspires me. Together, we will find the anchor in your storm.

As you embark on this voyage, take a moment to download the companion resources to this book by scanning the QR code below. Here you'll find a series of worksheets, exercise guides and other tools to help you take action on the strategies you'll find inside.

33dolphins.com/R3-book

To your success,

Paula

CONTENTS

Welcome to the Chaos   1

Act I: Rethink   **7**

Why You Need a Game Plan   9

Patterns in Chaos   17

When Emotions Are Your Enemy   25

Focus to Find Opportunity   37

Embrace Customer Obsession   45

Rethink Your Positioning   57

Act II: Realign   **77**

The Road Ahead   79

Build a High Impact Revenue Engine   81

Align Operations to Keep the Promise   95

Leverage Technology For Effectiveness and Innovation   109

8 Common Mistakes that Hinder Growth   125

Act III: Reinvent   **131**

Leadership Defines Your Future   133

Rebuild Confidence to Engage Your Market   137

Build a Crisis-Proof Business Model   147

From Crisis-Proof to Future-Ready   165

Conclusion: Turn Chaos into Opportunity   177

Bonus Materials & References   **179**

Chaos Patterns Over the Last Century   181

Notes   185

Acknowledgements   189

About the Author   190

Your Next Steps   191

When your business is facing a crisis, responding in ways that feel right almost guarantees your failure.

It doesn't have to.

WELCOME TO THE CHAOS

You're here because you have so much more at stake than your job. You're an entrepreneur. The stakes are higher for you.

You've poured your heart and soul into your business. It feeds your family, a family that includes your employees. You might even say that your business fulfills your purpose. It truly is a wonderful life, until it isn't. Then, it's terrifying.

When you're under stress, your human biology suddenly becomes your enemy. Unchecked, it will lead you to react in ways that block success and make your problems worse. That's why it's so easy to miss a shotgun just two inches to your left when you're facing down an angry bear.

Successful leaders know that overcoming this natural response is the key to not just surviving chaos, but navigating it so that you come out stronger. They have a game plan already in place that supports them to:

- Overcome their instincts and create the space to make better, more strategic choices when the stakes are high.
- Establish systems and processes that allow them to optimize for efficiency without hurting quality or cash flow.
- Automatically surface the opportunities that others overlook, so that they can act in ways that support growth.

You can become one of them.

My first lesson in navigating chaos came as a teenager watching my parents lose everything when the Canadian mining industry crashed in the late 80's. Back then, I optimistically believed they would get through it and everything would settle down. That's not quite how things worked out.

Everything didn't settle down. I started my professional life during the global recession of the early 90's, entered management at the dawn of the internet age, and started a business during the dot-com crash that followed. I've successfully steered that business through a banking crisis, massive globalization, and a pandemic. As I write this, we're facing yet another chaotic revolution driven by the overlapping effects from the dawn of the AI age, rising geopolitical unrest, and the threat of recession thanks to a global trade war.

Chaos is no longer the exception that proves the rule. It has become the rule. No sooner does one crisis end than a new one appears on the horizon. The frightening truth is that amidst all this uncertainty, we humans are wired to respond in ways that feel right but almost guarantee failure. It doesn't have to be this way.

This book will give you the tools you need to turn chaos into clarity and attain sustainable, customer-driven growth that keeps your business ahead, no matter what the market throws at you.

Chaos Is The New Normal

For a large swathe of the middle class, chaos has meant the steady erosion of their standard of living. And their dreams. Which is a real tragedy because the middle class happens to be where the seeds of the entrepreneurial spirit live. It's no wonder you sometimes feel as if the universe itself is conspiring against you.

What's truly eye opening? Some businesses thrive through all of this. They make money when times are good, and even more money when they're not. They're also a lot like yours. They don't have better products, smarter leaders, or some other magical advantage. They just make different decisions.

In times of chaos, two types of leaders emerge in every business:

- Those who hide in their offices (or behind a keyboard) pontificating disaster while throwing up their hands.
- Those who step up and get sh** done. Who accept the situation for what it is, and immediately get busy figuring out how make that work to their advantage.

You get to choose which type of leader you are going to become. If you choose to join the second group, this book has been written for you.

A Framework for Thriving, Not Just Surviving

The approach you are about to learn isn't about waiting out the storm. It's about **navigating** it. No fluffy motivational leadership speeches here — just practical, implementable strategies to help you take decisive, strategic action and capitalize on what's happening around you.

At its heart is a framework for growth designed to help you navigate chaos and come out ahead. When your world turns upside down, your outcomes depend entirely on your ability to:

- **Rethink** – So that your decisions are grounded in clarity.
- **Realign** – So that you stay relevant as your market changes.
- **Reinvent** – So that you're not just reacting to change, you're driving it.

Think of it as a three-legged stool. If you rely on just one or two pillars, your business risks toppling over. But when all three are in place, you create the stability to move forward, even in chaos.

I call this approach the Growth Architecture Framework, and it is the exact system I use to help my clients build businesses that are crisis-proof and future-ready.

The Growth Architecture Framework

How bold leaders build a business that is crisis-proof and future-ready.

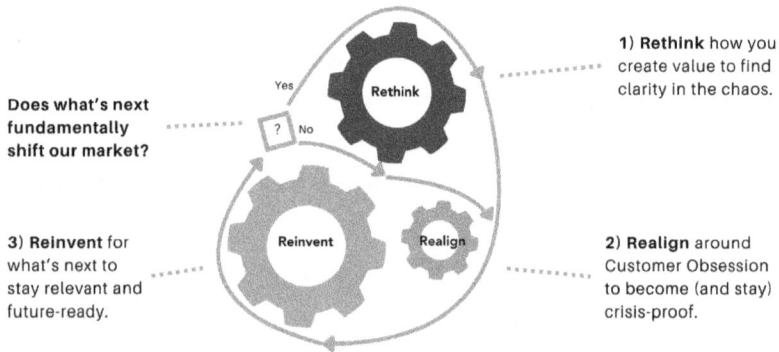

1) Rethink how you create value to find clarity in the chaos.

Rethink

Yes

? No

Does what's next fundamentally shift our market?

Reinvent

Realign

3) Reinvent for what's next to stay relevant and future-ready.

2) Realign around Customer Obsession to become (and stay) crisis-proof.

How To Get The Most From This Book

When I work with private clients, I bring all of my experience with me into the room every time we meet. Because of this, I'm able to tailor the structure of our work together to best fit their unique situation. I can't do that for you in this format, so I have deliberately crafted this book to let you use it in the way that best fits your current situation and preferred leadership style.

- *Act I: Rethink* grounds you in a strategic foundation to navigate chaos with clarity and confidence.
- *Act II: Realign* introduces practical systems to operationalize your vision and keep your team aligned around what matters most.
- *Act III: Reinvent* provides the forward-looking tools needed to sustain growth, no matter what the market throws your way.

Faced with an imminent crisis and not sure where to start?

You'll get the most value by working through the sections in this book in the order they're presented. Each Act addresses a specific aspect of implementing the Growth Architecture Framework and builds on the tools from the previous one in a logical sequence.

Fast-mover who wants to take action now and would rather skip the background details?

I got you. You don't need the theory. Start with the chapters *Embrace Customer Obsession* and *Rethink Your Positioning*, then jump right into Act's II and III in order. You can refer back to Act I any time you want to increase your grasp of the underlying theory or see a case example of the research that informs the Growth Architecture Framework.

Looking for growth and feeling pretty comfortable about where you're at right now?

Start by reading the chapter on Customer Obsession, then jump ahead to explore the ideas in *Act III: Reinvent* that show you how to ensure your business is crisis-proof and future-ready. You can then refer back to *Act I: Rethink* for more ideas on where to look for opportunity or *Act II: Realign* for insight on how to be sure you've put the right framework in place to support your goals.

Your Challenge

If you're holding this book, you're already questioning the status quo. That's a good sign. As we move through this journey together, I invite you to challenge your instincts. To lean into what works, even when it feels counterintuitive.

You don't have to navigate this storm alone. In the pages ahead, you'll find a roadmap, not just for surviving but for emerging stronger. The businesses that act now will be the ones that capture market share, build resilience, and set themselves up for long-term success.

Are you ready to be one of them?

ACT I: RETHINK

You can no more stop change than a piece of coal can choose not to become a diamond.

Author Unknown

1

WHY YOU NEED A GAME PLAN

Most of us start our entrepreneurial journey hoping we can sidestep chaos, fooling ourselves into believing that all we need are smart choices and good management. Then reality shows up, usually uninvited. Things don't go as smoothly as they were supposed to in your business plan. You're an entrepreneur though, so you own it. "This isn't working. It must be my fault - what am I doing wrong?"

Here's the secret you'll never read about in business books: chaos comes with the territory.

It can take years to finally accept this truth, and by then your self-confidence is diminished, often along with your financial situation.

In my decades-long career as an entrepreneur, I've survived a variety of chaotic moments:

- A broken water main flooded our offices, including our server room.

- A client defaulted on a payment equivalent to 3 months of operating overhead.

- A long-time client left us unexpectedly, signaling the start of a trend towards in-sourcing that put our core revenue streams at serious risk.

- An underground electrical fire forced us to evacuate our office with less than 12 minutes notice, and it would be 2 weeks before we could return.

Each time left me questioning my company's place in the world - our very right to exist. The flow of money through our business was disrupted and I had to rethink the foundational assumptions underpinning our business model.

When the COVID-19 pandemic hit in early 2020, I knew instantly that I needed a game plan and so did every one of my clients. I promise you this: whatever is happening in your firm that got you to pick up this book and read this far, you need one too. I'll also bet you a cup of coffee that you're thinking one of two things right now...

"I Already Have a Plan"

There are two types of leaders who say this:

Born Strategists:

You love strategy. I mean you *reeeally* love it.

The minute you saw the storm clouds forming on the horizon, you pulled out your existing, well-documented strategic plan, and began going through it with a highlighter, calling out all the areas that would need to be updated or re-evaluated in light of the current situation. Then you assigned team members to gather data to inform your next steps and report back - often with a pretty tight turnaround. Finally, you pulled your leadership team together, offered a clear, concise outline of the situation and its potential impacts, and guided your team (often with the help of a facilitator) through a structured process of mapping out your response.

If this is you, congratulations! You're well ahead of the game. As you work through the next few chapters, take a moment to ask "Did we consider this in crafting our plan?" Where your answer is no, revisit your thinking to be sure there isn't a hole in the assumptions underlying your strategy. If there is, the best time to address it is right now. You know what to do.

Casual Planners:

You have a plan... sort of.

Maybe it's in a binder that was delivered 2, 3, or 5 years ago by a consultant you haven't spoken to since. It could be an ad hoc collection of documents called "Strategy and Planning" or a collection of back-of-the-napkin doodles in your "great ideas" notebook. I have an entire bookshelf filled with those notebooks. When I die, there's a good chance my kids will use them to light the campfire. They're terrific kindling, not so helpful for organizing strategic thought. If this is you, I respectfully submit, what you're really saying is "I don't have time to plan. At least not a proper plan..." Keep reading.

"I Don't Have Time to Plan"

This is you if you have ever said "Planning is a waste of time." Or exclaimed in a meeting, "We need to take action, not sit around discussing strategy. We need to respond now!"

I've heard a lot of really smart leaders say things like this on our calls. They're action-oriented. They're determined to *do something. Do anything* just to feel like they're in control. It makes sense. Being action-oriented is a great way for a leader to be most of the time. The risk is that you will jump into action without really understanding the landscape, and when you do, the unintended consequences can be deadly.

I understand how you feel. Remember this *was* me. Here's the catch. What happens if, in 3 or 6 months' time, your actions have made things worse, not better? Will you have the time and resources to recover?

Why We Resist Planning

Stopping to develop a plan goes against the hustle ethos imbued in the romanticized notion we hold of the entrepreneurial spirit. Yet the fact is that the most important thing you can do to improve your chances of survival is to stop long enough to develop a game plan.

If you're like many of the driven entrepreneurs I work with, when you think about planning, you imagine hours cooped up in a stuffy room as the CEO drones on about their vision. Then everyone else talks about their contribution to that vision and commits to their quarterly or annual outcomes over stale donuts and weak coffee. It's the typical corporate retreat we've all come to expect.

While this work has its place in keeping your leadership team on the same page, it rarely leads to the kind of innovation you need right now. The plan I'm talking about comes before that step. It is the crucial piece of navigating uncertainty that is casually overlooked by most popular models for business growth.

A Note About Business Operating Systems

I frequently work with clients who have embraced popular business operating systems like EOS, Scaling Up, and OKRs. Despite having systemized processes and achieving operational discipline, they're struggling to grow. They tell me it feels like they're still treading water, just more efficiently.

There's a dirty secret no one tells you about most business operating systems. They optimize the systems, beliefs, and deliverables *that you already have*. They assume that you already have the strategy right and by simply continuing along the current path, just more efficiently and with less internal friction, you'll naturally grow. They work best under stable conditions, when you've already got growth architecture dialled in and your primary problem is managing complexity.

But if your business isn't already growing, you're not crystal clear on your ideal customer, or you haven't built your existing systems around serving their needs? You simply end up systemizing the suck. You're checking the boxes — holding daily huddles, tracking KPIs, setting your Rocks — but revenue stays flat and you're worn out from chasing new clients who never seem to convert.

Although their rigid structures have made them very popular with consultants and advisors from operations backgrounds, the challenge is that they tend to gloss over your go-to-market strategy. When your business isn't ready for operational optimization, the result is a gaping hole in your growth plan. Without a clear understanding of how customers find and choose you as their partner, you risk solving all the wrong problems for all the wrong people.

If you aren't already growing, your offer isn't nailed, or your sales process isn't dialled in, a business operating system won't fix it.

On the other side of the spectrum, acronyms like BANI[1] and VUCA[2] have become popular as useful tools to describe the complexity we find ourselves in, but they do very little to help you find your way through.

My goal here is not to name the storm. It is to help you gain traction inside it. This book will provide you with actionable tools to do just that.

The First Step, Rethink

Rethinking happens when you are willing to challenge your most closely held beliefs and consider the possibility that you've got it wrong. Rethinking is the fastest way to ensure that your decisions are grounded in clarity, not chaos.

It requires that you take a real pause. Step back from your business and assess the environmental variables that are impacting your situation. Are they permanent? Temporary? A signal of a larger restructuring? What is the impact on your customers? On *their* customers?

Only when you've gathered all of this information will you have the data points you need to establish a game plan that allows you to:

- Remain relevant as the situation changes.
- Strengthen your core in ways that do more than simply extend your runway.
- Capitalize on the new opportunities that inevitably follow a crisis.

In Act I, we'll look at the patterns that have emerged in each major economic crisis of the last century and explore what they mean for your situation right now. We'll have a frank conversation about how a crisis impacts your performance as a leader and how you can avoid the common mistakes that are literally hard-wired into human psychology. You'll choose what truths stand the test of time, and which beliefs to discard because they are no longer helpful. Finally, you'll get down to business and craft your statement of opportunity.

Your statement of opportunity clarifies how your business fits into the new reality that is emerging. It forms the foundation of the action plan you will develop in Act II: Realign. Let's get to it.

Download the Act I Templates

Be sure to scan the QR code to access free tools to help you implement the strategies inside.

33dolphins.com/R3-book

MEET ALEX: STUCK IN QUICKSAND

I'd like to introduce you to Alex. He's typical of the business leaders I work with and his story is one I've heard many times over the years. We'll check in with him throughout the book, to uncover how he used the principles you'll find here to turn his business around. But first you need to know where he started.

Alex owns a marketing agency that supports manufacturing companies & employs around 2 dozen people. Just a year ago, his business was solid with steady client contracts and a healthy sales pipeline. Then inflation started to spike and everything changed.

Inflation hit Alex's firm hard. They lost clients, contracts were cancelled, and project budgets were reduced. At networking events, he learned his competitors were experiencing the same things. Most were buckling down for what looked like a long, hard road ahead. So Alex made the hard decisions.

He froze hiring, slashed his own marketing budget, and focused on servicing existing clients rather than looking for new business. It was a defensive play that he believed would extend his runway and buy time for the market to recover.

At first, these measures *felt* like they were working as expenses went down and cash reserves stabilized. However, Alex's sales pipeline quickly dried up and his existing clients continued pulling back. With nothing to replace his lost sales, revenue plummeted. He described it as standing on quicksand where every move to save the business seemed to make things worse. In the coming chapters, we'll unpack what was really going on and what Alex missed.

2

PATTERNS IN CHAOS

Your ability to recognize the patterns that live inside chaos is like having a magic key that unlocks prosperity and stability in your business. It's also easier than you think.

For as long as there have been businesses, entrepreneurs have been challenged and disrupted by crises. While each one has unique causes, consistent patterns occur in the way both markets and businesses respond. By looking at how those responses historically shaped business recovery, you can better predict how your decisions today will play out over the long term. You will know exactly how to position your business to survive the crisis and emerge stronger.

The first pattern to recognize is that chaos rarely results from a single event. More often, forces unexpectedly collide to destabilize the existing economic order. Some of these forces are predictable, while others are sudden and disruptive. Almost all of them are entirely beyond your control. This is true whether the uncertainty you're facing right now is global or isolated to your industry, your city, or even your business.

Now for the good news. No matter what triggers a crisis, its impact is anything but random. This means that once you understand which forces are driving what's happening around you, you have the power to make better decisions. Instead of feeling blindsided by uncertainty, you'll anticipate shifts and take corrective action before your business is irreparably harmed.

Forces That Drive Chaos

These impacts fall into one of four buckets and there is usually more than one bucket in play for any given crisis. As you read through them, which ones do you identify with? These are clues to the forces impacting your situation today.

Globalization & Trade Disruptions

Modern economies are tightly interconnected. This means that what happens on the other side of the world often has immediate consequences here at home. Trade wars, tariffs, and supply chain disruptions will make it harder for businesses to predict costs or secure materials. If your business relies too heavily on one region for either supplies or exports, you may find yourself in a vulnerable position when these events happen.

Conversely, the ability of global competitors to access your local market can put pressure on pricing that squeezes your margins. Remote work has made it possible for many businesses to hire employees from an offshore labor pool that is generally available at lower wages. The resulting operating imbalance can lead to price pressure, making it harder for locally staffed competitors to stay profitable.

Technological Disruptions

Since the invention of the printing press, technological innovation has been a precursor to rapid economic change. Even though recent advances like AI and automation are transforming entire industries at breakneck speed, the impacts of technology are predictable: efficiency, cost reduction, access to knowledge, and innovative new revenue streams.

Fail to take advantage of new technologies and you will eventually become obsolete, but jumping into every new trend becomes a never-ending game of whack-a-mole. It is the leaders who embrace technology purposefully that are most likely to gain a market advantage. Your challenge will be choosing when and what technology to integrate into your business without getting caught up in hype-driven distractions.

Government Policies & Economic Shifts

Interest rates, taxation, and regulation will always be a factor your business must grapple with. However, sometimes government policies contribute to, rather than improve, the crisis. The irony is that these policies are usually enacted in response to an existing challenge and their effectiveness varies widely.

For example, the Smoot-Hawley Tariff Act of 1930[3] is widely credited with making the Great Depression much worse, not just in America but worldwide. Just three years later, the New Deal kicked off a decade-long rollout of social programs, financial reforms and infrastructure projects credited with driving recovery in the USA. How your government responds will have a significant role in shaping the magnitude of the chaos you are facing.

Changing Consumer Behavior

Consumer behavior generally changes in response to movement in the other buckets. Not only are the changes predictable, they may be your most visible indicator that the winds have changed. Chaotic events have a tendency to alter spending habits. In uncertain times, consumers become more selective, prioritizing essential goods and services while cutting back on anything they deem as non-essential. This is also true of business spending. During a crisis period, understanding how your customer's psychology is changing is crucial to your survival. It's even more important than managing your finances.

Of course these drivers are only part of the story. How businesses respond in times of economic uncertainty is what separates those that thrive from those that don't.

How Markets Respond

We can look to the major economic crises of the last 100 years for clues about what to expect when chaos hits. From the Great Depression to the COVID-19 pandemic, the markets have reacted in the following ways (see Bonus Materials for detailed event notes and sources).

Financial markets are inherently fragile.

Market vulnerability exists long before a downturn appears, but it is dormant, hiding in the shadows. Then some trigger event causes an unexpected downturn and the market vulnerability is exposed or even amplified. A great example of this is the 2008 financial crisis. When the US housing market collapsed, it revealed predatory lending practices that had left the banking system exposed to massive losses. The resulting shockwaves were intense, sparking a global financial crisis. The markets responded by making regulatory changes aimed at restoring investor and consumer confidence. Those changes are likely to impact your access to capital and the rules your business must operate under.

Governments respond to stimulate recovery.

Stimulus packages and relief measures provide temporary lifelines, but often bring unwelcome long-term consequences you're already familiar with. Think of the one-two punch of high inflation and increased national debt experienced by every country following the COVID-19 pandemic. Costs went up, funding for social programs was reduced, and taxation increased. Following a period of heavy stimulus, your business often gets squeezed from both ends. Buyer price sensitivity increases at the same time as your input costs are going up. This is why waiting for government intervention to "fix" the economy is so often a fatal mistake. Hoping for a bailout can mean you wait too long to take meaningful action.

Social systems are strained.

Less money moving through the economy often means an increase in both food and housing insecurity, driven by rising unemployment. Frustrated citizens desperate for a lifeline and struggling to make ends meet reduce spending, which lowers demand for what you sell. Property crime might go up. The search for employment increases migration, permanently changing the social structure of communities. Meanwhile, added stress leaves families more prone to divorce or abuse.

When these conditions are allowed to fester, societies become susceptible to extremist or populist views and policies. As a business leader, this impacts your ability to hire the talent you need, manage your insurance rates, and even maintain your corporate culture.

How Business Responds

When a crisis hits, all leaders make a series of difficult choices. In practical terms, your options are limited. It's inevitable that you will use some combination of these four responses.

- **Cost-Cutting Measures**: You can try to preserve cashflow by reducing your expenses. This usually involves laying off employees, cancelling contracts, scaling back marketing, or halting expansion plans.

- **Operational Streamlining**: Without ready cash to invest in growth, you may strive to optimize operations, renegotiate supplier contracts, reduce perceived waste, or invest in other efficiency improvements to weather a downturn.

- **Diversification & Pivoting**: Looking for new sources of revenue, you may pivot your business model, target new customer segments, or leverage existing assets differently.

- **Leveraging Digital Transformation**: As technology has revolutionized the way business gets done, many companies are motivated by crisis to embrace digital transformations in a bid to maintain or even grow market share.

You will either make decisions designed to build a moat around what you have or you will make strategic adjustments in a bid to stay ahead. No matter which camp you fall into, some defensive action is often necessary.

Most leaders intuitively try to do more while using fewer resources. In a bid to preserve profit margins, they place their focus on cost cutting and operational efficiency. On the surface, this makes sense. History teaches us it isn't quite true.

This approach is likely to leave your business starved of both the human and capital resources needed to pursue opportunities for growth. There is a better model, and it's backed by research.

You will come through the storm stronger if you take proactive steps to adapt and innovate. The data shows that businesses who pivot, embrace technology, and respond proactively to shifting market needs have significantly better outcomes following a crisis.

In *Roaring Out of Recession*, Harvard Business Review[4] revealed how companies following a specific recipe consistently outperform all others coming out of a downturn. They strategically balance operational efficiency with workforce development, while making targeted investments in sales and marketing. Those that rely solely on protectionist measures rarely regain their former market position. Leaning deeply into cost-cutting and retreat during a crisis guarantees that you will struggle to recover.

I have recognized this same pattern at play in my work with clients. The ones that embrace a foundation of customer obsession to combine strategically optimized operations and digital transformation with proactive sales and marketing consistently outperform those who focus on minimizing costs to maintain profit. Obsessing over quarterly numbers and driving financial metrics above all else is supposed to make your business more successful. In a crisis, it can cause your business to wither and die.

The most stunning pattern that emerged from the research floored me. When you really look at what's underneath the business community's defensive posture, you realize that the culprit isn't just fear. It's our insistence on using revenue as the measurement by which we quantify success. When your sole focus is on *revenue and profit in this moment*, you're so busy staring at your feet that you can't see the road ahead.

It doesn't matter how big or small your company is. Even well-respected brands with significant resources had very different outcomes following the banking crisis of 2007-2009.

Sony, once an unbeatable electronics powerhouse, cut costs and delayed planned R&D investments. By the time Kazuo Hirai took the reins in 2012, Sony had lost significant market share and its competitive edge. Major restructuring was needed to improve the company's outlook and they are still trying to fully regain their pre-2007 market share almost 20 years later[5].

At the same time, Apple prioritized "investing our way through" according to co-founder Steve Jobs. He refused to consider layoffs and increased the company's R&D budget, moves that led to the release of the iPad just two years later[6]. Apple embraced customer obsession over financial obsession, optimizing their revenue engine to meet customers where they were at. By the time the recession was over, Apple was still dominating the mobile phone market and maintaining a loyal and growing presence in the personal computer space — a position they still enjoy to this day.

Sony survived their mistakes but the outcomes are much less rosy for most companies. Small businesses who lose momentum during a downturn are likely to find themselves without the resources they need for the kind of reinvention Kazuo Hirai undertook at Sony. Too often, the finale is either closing your business or selling what's left to a financially stronger buyer. But knowledge is power.

Now that you can see the patterns that drive success, you have the ability to choose differently. In the next chapter, you will come to understand the societal conditioning that drives your instinctive reactions and gain the tools to change them.

Key Takeaways

Take a moment now to think about your own responses to past crises. How do your choices compare to those of the businesses in this chapter? Have you ever forgone long-term stability to secure short-term financial performance?

To build a truly sustainable business that will fund your future, your response now must take these realities into account:

- Businesses that focus on short-term survival often struggle to regain momentum after a crisis.
- Investing in innovation, digital transformation, and customer retention helps businesses emerge stronger.
- Agility and adaptability, rather than extreme cost-cutting, are the defining traits of businesses that thrive in economic turbulence.

3

WHEN EMOTIONS ARE YOUR ENEMY

When I was looking at the results my clients had achieved coming out of their own crises, I noticed another pattern emerging. This one was a real game-changer. The biggest hurdles most of them faced came from internal forces working against their success, not the external forces driving the crisis. I'm a bit of a nerd, so I had to figure out why.

The businesses who struggled were no different than the ones that thrived. Their leaders were equally smart, equally talented, and equally passionate. They were good people who had assembled skilled teams that delivered exceptional products and services to their clients. They truly cared about, and took pride in, their work. They may even have been targeting the exact same customers with almost identical offers and very similar pricing. So what was the difference?

I discovered that even the best business strategy falters under pressure when fear and stress are driving the bus.

It turns out that when faced with uncertainty, the human brain automatically defaults to survival mode. Focusing on short-term relief rather than long-term strategy is an instinctive part of our evolutionary psyche. Three things happen in your brain the instant you face an imminent threat:

- **Fear makes you play it safe**. When you are trapped in survival mode, you will naturally become so obsessed with avoiding the losses that you completely miss the potential gains.

- **Stress gives you tunnel vision**. Your mind focuses on the things you are stressed about, narrowing your field of perception and limiting your creative thinking. This leads to quick but reactive decisions that don't take the big-picture into account.

- **Action makes you feel like you've taken control**. Taking action, any action, feels better than sitting in uncertainty, even if it's the wrong move.

Sometimes referred to as the psychology of crisis leadership, this happens to every single one of us. It is also the reason so many business owners continue to make the same mistakes time and time again, even though we know better. Feeling as though our very survival is threatened, we instinctively respond by cutting too deep, retreating from the market, and making reactive choices instead of strategic ones.

The biggest difference between the clients who thrived and the ones who barely survived a downturn was simply this: The ones who thrived made a conscious effort to overcome their instinctive reactions. Your challenge is to do the same.

How Innate Biases Hinder You

Unchecked, these three innate cognitive biases will pop up to derail your thinking and cause you to make poor decisions[7]. They're mental shortcuts that help us process information quickly, influencing how we perceive and respond to challenges. Useful when we're running from a grizzly, they're dangerous in high-pressure business situations.

Understanding how these biases influence you is the first step toward overcoming them and making sound strategic decisions.

- **Fear is driven by loss aversion.** It causes you to focus more attention on avoiding losses than finding opportunity. It's at play when you instantly look to cut marketing and innovation budgets, delay necessary investments, or cling stubbornly to failing business models. Overcoming this fear requires a shift in perspective. Rather than focusing on what could be lost, consider the opportunity cost of doing nothing. What are you losing by playing it too safe?

- **Groupthink** is a stress response. It occurs when you blindly follow industry trends or competitors without questioning whether those moves are right for your own business. When others are cutting costs aggressively or making drastic shifts, it feels safer to do the same. Feels safer, but is usually dangerous. Now is the time to ask more critical questions, seek independent data, and encourage diverse perspectives within your teams to avoid echo chambers. Thinking differently is the best competitive advantage you can have in uncertain times.

- **Action bias** pushes you to make fast decisions simply for the sake of doing something, even when waiting or inaction would be the wiser choice. Simply put, it feels better to act, even when that action is ill-advised. In a crisis, the impulse to react quickly can lead to rash layoffs, untested pivots, or overcorrections that create instability. The antidote is to implement a pause-and-assess rule. Force yourself to consider whether a decision is truly strategic or simply a knee-jerk reaction to fear. Sometimes, the best move is patience.

When these biases are all at work, they lead you to focus on holding on to what you have. The main question becomes "Can we get by without this?" Unsure what's coming, you look around for clues and see your competitors and your clients cutting back and laying off. Today, you might see them bragging about replacing their workers with armies of AI agents. This deepens your fear. You need to do something to feel in control. So you naturally cut costs and eliminate any non-essential spending, while delaying major investments until things get better.

Successful leaders experience all of these biases too. They just don't let them drive. They know that in order to turn things around, they need to do more than simply recognize when their decision-making is coming from a place of fear. One of the defining traits in leaders who steer their businesses successfully through a crisis is that they take ownership of their reactions and manage their emotions, so that they can capitalize on the opportunities before them to build a crisis-proof business.

Emotional Intelligence: Your Superpower to Overcome Biases

You're going to need more than awareness to outsmart Mother Nature. Awareness is simply the first step toward preventing yourself from making costly mistakes. It will take discipline to think clearly under pressure and manage your emotions, all while keeping your team engaged. You need a reliable way to take back control as soon as you recognize that fear is in the driver's seat.

In her book, The Emotionally Strong Leader[8], Carolyn Stern points out that strong leaders aren't immune to stress. They simply know how to process it without letting it dictate their decisions. Carolyn reassures us that emotional control isn't about avoiding your emotions, it's about embracing them without letting them takeover.

When you can stay calm and centered, you'll assess situations objectively and execute strategic moves while others are paralyzed by fear. This ability is an important byproduct of developing strong emotional intelligence. Cultivating it will allow you to navigate uncertainty with a steady hand rather than a trembling one. You can do it. In fact you must.

Business owners who learn to regulate their emotions and recognize stress triggers make far better decisions than those who react impulsively. They use emotions as data points that help them recognize when a decision is important or risky, rather than letting emotions control their actions.

How Emotional Intelligence Mattered in the COVID-19 Pandemic

The COVID-19 pandemic tested business leaders like never before. The ones who demonstrated emotional intelligence were able to make strategic moves that set them apart.

Take Shopify, for example. Instead of retreating, they doubled down on supporting small businesses by offering extended free trials and additional resources to retailers moving their stores online. By the end of 2021, annual revenue had nearly tripled[9] to $4.61B.

Their leadership team's ability to stay focused on the bigger picture allowed them to capitalize on customer needs and come through the pandemic stronger than before. But it wasn't only technology firms that made these moves.

Canadian hotelier Accent Inns leaned into their renowned creativity to strengthen their brand at a time when competitors were facing financial ruin. The family-owned company operates both the Hotel Zed and Accent Inns hotel chains in my home province of British Columbia. They used their unique position to support front-line health care workers by offering a safe, comfortable place to stay that would protect their families from being exposed to secondary infection. It was a move that was at once brilliantly on-brand and wildly innovative. Accent Inns became part of the fight, gaining the kind of respect and loyalty that lasts well beyond a crisis. In the process, they gained national media attention[10].

Two companies, in very different industries, with different response strategies and a common goal — to fight instinct so that they could see the unexpected opportunity in the moment before them. If they could do it, why can't you?

5 Core Traits of Emotionally Strong Leaders

The most effective crisis leaders I've met have the following traits:

1. They recognize the personal triggers and biases that cloud their judgment.
2. They manage their emotional responses to avoid rash, reactive decisions.
3. They are willing to adjust strategies based on new data rather than stubbornly clinging to outdated plans.
4. They proactively stay connected to how employees and customers are feeling, building stability and trust.
5. They recognize when to act boldly and when to hold steady, and actively avoid making moves out of fear.

These traits help them better lead their teams though chaos by preventing reactive decision-making and resisting the urge to overcorrect, ensuring morale stays strong.

Managing your emotions isn't about becoming cold or detached. In fact, it's the opposite. It's the secret to becoming a more effective leader who can handle crisis moments without making things worse.

What to Do When Fear is in the Driver's Seat

Just because these reactions are natural doesn't mean the mistakes they cause are inevitable. Recognizing your cognitive biases gives you the power to build checkpoints into your decision-making and override emotional reactions to prevent bias from sabotaging your success.

You can move from defense to offense by learning to see uncertainty as a catalyst for change, rather than a threat.

A rare few grow up with a natural tendency to think this way. They default to a proactive coping method. Others develop a more self-protective approach. Take a moment now to examine your own default setting.

When chaos hits, do you tend to fall into a:

- **Survival Mindset:** Leaders with this mindset immediately cut costs, freeze hiring, and delay decisions. The impact? Slowing momentum, loss of talent, and possibly reduced market relevance.

- **Opportunity Mindset:** These leaders focus their energy to optimize efficiency, invest in new capabilities, and reposition their business to meet their customers where they're at. This approach often leads to increased market share and long-term resilience.

It's important to be honest with yourself. Your ability to adapt starts with how you frame your situation and even though your default patterns are set in childhood, you *can* change them.

You might think I was born seeing opportunity around every corner. I wasn't. I was born in Northern Ireland in the middle of the Troubles, to parents who had started life during the Great Depression. We came to Canada when I was just 4 years old, leaving everything and everyone I knew behind. Survival mindset is hardwired into my genes. It's taken work and discipline to flip the switch so that I consciously look for opportunity in chaos. It may never come naturally, but I've learned to recognize the warning signs and proactively shift my perspective. The first step was to make a commitment to myself that I would not let my past define my future. I invite you to do the same thing right now.

Simply by stepping back and questioning your impulsive reactions, you can make a conscious choice to shift from reactive decision-making to strategic resilience. You can't control external chaos, but you can control how you respond to it. Strengthening your resilience as a leader means developing systems that support you in avoiding fear-based decisions and reinforce strategic thinking. In my work with clients, I use these practical strategies to help them find clarity amid chaos:

- **Build a crisis playbook.** Leaders who plan for uncertainty are less likely to be blindsided when disruptions hit. Set aside time to identify potential risks and create response strategies during your annual and quarterly planning activities. In her book Imaginable[11], author Jane McGonigal demonstrates this effect when she describes how study participants tasked with living through an imaginary pandemic experienced much less stress than the average citizen when COVID-19 hit the world in 2020.
- **Develop a crisis decision framework.** Set clear criteria for when to act versus when to wait. Defining a framework for action before a crisis arrives ensures that your decisions are driven by logic, not impulse.
- **Practice mental distancing.** When facing a tough decision, ask "What advice would I give a friend in my position?" Creating psychological distance between yourself and the problem reduces emotional reactivity and improves clarity.

4 Questions to Re-orient Your Thinking

Since you're reading this book, I'm guessing that you don't have a crisis playbook and a crisis decision framework handily tucked away on a shelf just waiting for you to need it. That was certainly true for me, and it's been true for almost all of my clients.

When facing a crisis unprepared, we use these four questions to recognize when emotion is driving critical choices. Any time you feel fear or panic burbling up inside you, pause and consciously assess:

1. Am I making this decision to feel safer, or because it's the best long-term move?
2. What data supports this action?
3. What are the best and worst case scenarios if I do this?
4. Is there any evidence from past crises that guarantees this will be successful?

It's also helpful to have a routine that helps you calm your fears and gives you time to reflect from a calmer place. The routines that work best are different for everyone, and you may have to try a few different strategies to find one that works for you.

One leader I know doesn't make any decision until she's slept on it. That means no more late-night emails to the team to share your latest, greatest idea. Leave that email in draft until morning and revisit it again before hitting send.

Another practices mindfulness, taking a 15-minute pause to meditate between making a high-pressure decision and sharing or acting on it.

Yet another takes a solo walk in the park near his office, letting the exercise help him work out any nerves while he makes sure he can answer the questions above.

I have many clients who regularly call me up when they're facing a new challenge, just to talk through the options they're considering and help them think through the consequences. They know I'll ask the tough questions and trust that I have their best interests at heart.

4 Steps to Pivot from Fear to Strategic Growth

Once you recognize that you're battling the forces of evolution and acknowledged that your thinking has been fear-based, your next step is to move your thought process from fear of loss to a focus on the possibility of strategic growth. It's actually a whole lot easier than it sounds.

Start by listing the things you believe are happening - that people aren't buying, that AI is making you obsolete, that you don't have the right connections, that a well-known competitor "owns" the market. Whatever it is, call it out in black and white.

Next, assume you're wrong, then go looking for evidence that proves it. When you find it, you have your answer.

Now have the courage to let go of what's been lost and create space for what's to come. Every crisis creates demand shifts. Your job now is to find them by looking forward, not back. Which brings us to step four.

Give yourself permission to think outside the box for opportunities to repurpose what you already have in ways your competitors have overlooked. You might find an untapped market for existing products, or entirely new needs that your experience and skills are perfectly positioned to solve.

Take your time with these questions. Don't rush them. When I'm working one on one with a client and their leadership team, I take them through a series of exercises designed to challenge assumptions and surface opportunities in a workshop that lasts for half a day. If you're doing this alone, you might find it easier to sit with each question for an hour (or a day) before moving on to the next. You'll be surprised at what comes up.

A Word of Encouragement

Whatever situation you're facing right now, I know it's scary. I know because I've been there. I've sacrificed family holidays because the business needed me present. Worked weekends and pulled overnighters to do the jobs of three people just to get the ball rolling. Wakened up at 3 am with cold fingers of dread squeezing my stomach, my brain still on fire with the worry that made it so hard to fall asleep just hours earlier. I've put on a fake smile and fake confidence heading into a sales call with a prospect I desperately needed to close and congratulated a pivotal employee on a fabulous new role while my brain frantically tried to internalize a vision of my business without them.

I can also tell you this. Not one single time did responding from that place of fear do anything but make my problems exponentially worse. Only by flipping the switch on that nagging dread have I ever been able to turn the ship around and sail into recovery. Fortunately, once I figured out how to flip the switch quickly and reliably, business got a whole lot easier.

In the next chapter, you'll learn how to recognize opportunities and decide on the strategic moves that will position your business for long-term success. Armed with new insight, you'll be ready to start crafting your game plan in Act II: Realign.

Key Takeaway: Leadership in Crisis Is a Choice

1. Economic turbulence is inevitable. You control how you respond to it.
2. Businesses don't fail because of market conditions. They fail because their leaders make decisions based on fear instead of strategy.
3. Great leaders survive chaos simply by refusing to retreat. They resist panic, challenge their biases, and make strategic moves even when fear tells them otherwise.

4

FOCUS TO FIND OPPORTUNITY

Where you place your attention is also where you birth your results. While most businesses are focused on simply surviving the crisis, you can use it as a launchpad for new opportunities. Let uncertainty become your doorway to lasting competitive advantage by approaching it with the right perspective.

Resilient leaders look for ways to capitalize on shifting conditions, spotting gaps in the market and making moves their competitors are too afraid to take. Struggling leaders try to avoid mistakes instead of actively seeking the opportunities hiding in uncertainty.

Sounds simple, doesn't it?

It is simple, but that doesn't mean it's either easy or obvious. Act too fast, and you'll always be one step ahead of the market. Too slow, and you'll always be chasing someone else's tail lights. To win at this game, you will need to train your mind to pay attention to the gaps, to listen differently to your customers, and to fiercely manage your own fear. You're going to need a simple method for recognizing a golden opportunity at exactly the right time, so that you can grab on before it passes you by.

Think of this journey like hunting for Easter Eggs as a kid — you know they're there, you just have to find them. And the hunt is half the fun. Let's dig in!

What's Changing and Where Can You Win?

Every crisis you encounter will reshape your market in some way. Shifting priorities often expose gaps or weaknesses that were previously unimportant. What your customers want and need, how they set priorities, how they buy, how they make decisions and what they worry about will all transform.

Their spending doesn't stop, but it does change. That's what makes it so complicated to tease out the solvable pain amidst the noise.

Think back to the early days of COVID-19. Restaurants were forced to close overnight and many owners feared it was the end of their businesses. Meanwhile, customers trapped at home still wanted relief from the chore of cooking daily meals. An entirely new food service model quickly emerged — kitchens offering both make-at-home and hot-cooked meals for delivery through popular apps like SkiptheDishes or Doordash. The pandemic is now behind us, but that new model is still thriving today.

As you are considering what's changing in your industry, here are some common behavioral clues I've observed along with suggestions on how you might respond.

Buying Behavior Shifts

During a crisis, both businesses and consumers tend to become more selective. You may see your customers prioritizing cost-effective, high-value solutions over both luxury goods and cheap disposable items. They are re-evaluating your value using entirely new criteria.

When this happens, look for opportunities to help them in new ways that save time, solve priority problems, or navigate the uncertainty. These are often places where you can gain an edge to retain the business.

Acknowledging that the way they perceive your value has changed, then demonstrating how your service aligns with their new priorities while also offering more flexible financing or payment terms may be the ticket to retaining more of your core customer base.

Cost Cutting Becomes a Priority

Customers seeking to reduce overhead will cut inefficiencies, automate tasks, and streamline operations. When this happens, you might be asked for price reductions, more favorable payment terms, or even contract cancellations and buy-outs. At the same time, technology solutions often see increased demand in these environments as companies look to do more with less. You're in a strong position if your business can help companies optimize spending without sacrificing performance.

Supply Chains Falter

Broken supply chains leave businesses scrambling for the raw materials they need to deliver their goods and services to customers. The struggle can be amplified by government responses like tariffs, embargos, and sanctions. When you step up where the default solution is faltering, you can gain a long-term competitive advantage. Could you offer flexible sourcing, localized production, or faster delivery alternatives? Services firms may find that companies suddenly prefer to work with partners closer to home, or need to shift relationships away from riskier regions to more politically stable areas.

Look no further than the strong "Buy Canadian" sentiment that emerged in response to the 2025 tariff policies introduced by the US Government for evidence of this outcome in action. Overnight, supply chains became a factor in even the smallest buying decision at the grocery store and an entire industry emerged helping Canadian shoppers buy local. Within 6 months, new shopping apps emerged, "Made in Canada" labels were everywhere, packaging was redesigned, and entirely new food production businesses took hold.

Interest in Digital Solutions Accelerates

Economic pressure forces even the most reluctant industries to modernize. This leads to rapid adoption of technologies that may previously have been considered too risky. E-commerce, cloud computing, and cybersecurity solutions have all experienced surges in demand as businesses have pivoted to digital-first models. More recently, the rising popularity of AI has companies looking for help to build AI agents for the very first time.

What problems are created by the rapid adoption of something new? Can your firm provide targeted industry training to help smooth out the bumps that inevitably accompany new tech platforms? When your business can help clients better adopt new technology, automate repetitive tasks, improve security, or enhance remote work capabilities, you'll be in high demand.

Financial and Risk Management Takes Priority

Uncertainty makes all businesses more risk-averse and, at the same time, more eager for guidance. Financial consultants, risk management advisors, and alternative funding providers become essential resources. If you have expertise in financial strategy, cash flow management, or alternative financing, businesses will seek out your insights during these times. The same is true for legal support to help with contract cancellations, bad debt collections, and liquidation firms.

Relationships Become Fluid

Commitment-heavy relationship models struggle amid chaos. Subscription-based, pay-as-you-go, and other flexible pricing models become more attractive as companies prioritize cash flow over large capital expenditures or long-term commitments.

If you can adjust your pricing model to reduce risk for your customers, you'll gain a competitive edge. Consider replacing high up-front fees with smaller, more frequent payments, or developing a series of shorter engagement offers that deliver laser-focused, high-impact solutions and quick ROI rather than bundling everything into a one-year commitment.

Not All Opportunities Are Equal

By now, you've very likely come up with several different ideas to meet your customers and prospects where they're at. And as a bold entrepreneur, you're likely chomping at the bit to take action. Don't. At least, not yet.

You have an opportunity to build a lasting competitive advantage that will deliver value long after the current crisis is over. It's critical to pause long enough to evaluate which kinds of opportunity you're facing, so that you can focus your attention on the ones with the most potential.

There is a temporary shift in the market.

A short term need arises for something that isn't usually important, and that won't be important once the current situation has passed. Remember the stylish facemasks that were sold during the COVID-19 pandemic? Cloth masks that expressed your personal style were everywhere you went with some prices reaching $50 or more. For a short period of time, you could make a pretty decent profit off what was literally a few dollars-worth of fabric and labor. But the runway was short. Pivoting to serve this type of shift only makes sense if you can do so easily as a way to boost revenues until demand for your core products rebounds.

Rising demand for existing product that's likely to survive the moment.

Sometimes a crisis changes consumer behavior in a way that makes something old and familiar wildly more popular. You're probably familiar with how COVID triggered sudden acceptance of remote work, creating huge demand for virtual meetings. By then, tools like Zoom had been around for nearly a decade and were used mostly by early tech adopters. With almost everyone now working remotely, teams began holding regular virtual meetings. Staff appreciated not having to battle traffic in order to meet face to face. Companies saved money by gaining back the productivity of those once wasted travel hours not to mention the cost savings associated with less travel. As COVID restrictions were removed, employees resisted the return to in-person work and remote work became a permanent part of corporate life. Companies who refused to embrace this reality quickly faced backlash of varying degrees.

An entirely new category emerges.

Staying with the COVID theme, virtual meetings collided with the rise of artificial intelligence, yielding a new market for AI-powered meeting assistants that made notetaking much easier and orders of magnitude more accurate. I have actually been in meetings where more notetakers showed up than actual people! This was unheard of before COVID and unimaginable to live without today. Technology companies that were able to recognize the opportunity to create tools that enhanced virtual meetings and act on that knowledge benefitted from this new category.

Prioritize options that offer sustainable advantage by delivering long-term value. These are the opportunities that are likely to survive the current moment. Both AI-tools and online meeting platforms continue to be profitable businesses today, while the demand for facemasks has almost disappeared alongside the threat of COVID. It only makes sense to jump on a temporary market shift if doing so bridges short-term cash flow needs and helps you either build a bridge to a more sustainable pivot or allows you to survive until guaranteed demand for your core product recovers once the current storm passes.

Your Mission, Should You Choose to Accept It

I hope by now you've accepted that you don't control the chaos, but you do control how you respond to it.

- You've gained a new understanding of the predictable patterns that accompany crises and how those patterns light the path to a stronger future for your business.

- You know how human psychology can work against you by nudging you to make short-sighted, fear-based choices that weaken your business.

- You've learned how to manage your instinctive emotional reactions to the threat chaos poses and where to focus your attention to recognize the opportunities around you.

Your challenge now is to find the courage you will need to adapt faster than your competitors and gain lasting advantage. If you're up for the challenge, I'm here to walk beside you on the path. Let's keep moving forward, together.

YOUR TURN: STEP INTO ALEX'S SHOES

Let's check in on our old friend Alex, the business owner we met at the start of this book. Now that you understand the psychology that drives us in times of stress, you can recognize how fear and panic fed into Alex's early decision-making. His reaction is a textbook case of cognitive bias at work.

- Loss aversion drove him to focus on avoiding financial losses more than gaining opportunities, while ignoring the long-term damage his actions would cause.
- Action bias compelled him to make and act quickly on decisions instead of taking time to assess the situation strategically.
- Groupthink reinforced these choices. Alex assumed following his peers was his best move without questioning if they were right.

Before you continue, take a moment to imagine you're Alex. You've started to recognize that your initial response to the crisis wasn't strategic. It was emotional. The actions you took gave you a sense of control in the moment, but they're now creating deeper problems. Your competitors are gaining market share, your team is disengaged, and your pipeline is drying up. What would you recommend Alex do next?

Take note of your answers and compare them to the strategies we'll discuss in the pages that follow. By thinking critically about these choices now, you'll be better prepared to avoid the same pitfalls in your own leadership.

5

EMBRACE CUSTOMER OBSESSION

Now that you've identified what opportunities are emerging, you need a way to connect them to your business. You need a lighthouse — a beacon that reliably points you in the right direction and helps you steer clear of hazards, even when the horizon is obscured by the dense fog of confusion. That lighthouse is your strategic opportunity statement, and the way you find it is through customer obsession.

Customer obsession lives at the intersection of empathy with your customer's reality and your commitment to proactively anticipating and adapting to their changing needs. You will use personal insights supported by market intelligence and a repeatable system for continually refreshing your understanding of the community you serve.

Over time, your focus on customer obsession will deliver a cultural shift in your business where you are continually working to understand what's changing in your customers' worlds and using that insight to adjust your own strategy in real time.

My Hardest Lesson

It's easy to believe that once you've built a relationship with a new customer, the hard work is finished. But discovery doesn't end with the first sale. Even the most established businesses will lose touch if they stop paying attention to the shifting dynamics around them. It's the reason that 52% of Fortune 500 businesses have disappeared within the last 20 years[12].

After successfully running my digital marketing agency in Vancouver for more than two decades, I thought I knew my customers inside and out. Still, I couldn't shake a vague sense of unease. Let me tell you how that situation unfolded, and how it ultimately shaped the way I think about staying close to your customers.

My agency was respected and successful. We had long-term clients who had stayed with us for 8 to 12 years. Some days it felt like I was the longest serving member their revenue team. New sales or marketing leaders would frequently call: "Hey Paula, we have a new project we're planning and the boss says we did something similar in 2008. Any chance you've got documentation on that?"

Nine times out of ten, we did. Thanks to strong systems and operational discipline, we could usually find the creative briefs, artwork, and project metrics in under half an hour. Clients were always impressed and we'd be invited to lead the project a second time. Sounds amazing right?

Wrong.

Price pressure from those legacy clients grew more and more intense. Even as we consistently outperformed our competitors, they demanded more and deeper discounts. Our familiarity was viewed as a reason to charge less, not value worth a premium fee. The constant pressure was capping our revenue, squeezing our margins, and eroding our ability to invest in our future.

I felt trapped. And I did all the wrong things. I cut costs, scaled back our marketing budget, and retrenched to founder-led sales. I managed cash flow and monitored utilization rates with the obsession of a new parent. Meanwhile less efficient competitors were charging significantly more and growing faster. I couldn't understand it. It was also pissing me off.

My frustration came to head in a meeting with the procurement team for one of our key clients. Our contact had called me in to negotiate yet another price break. After asking about other similar vendors, I learned something shocking. Those vendors were taking longer to deliver work that was less accurate and achieving inferior results. Yet they were charging 4x what we were, for the exact same work.

I turned to the procurement officer, "We're faster, more accurate, and deliver higher value at a lower fee...?"

He nodded. "I'm curious... why am I here?"

He didn't know. Neither did our sponsor.

I would love to tell you that the client realized our value, quadrupled our fees, and took work away from our competitors. But this isn't a fairytale.

In the real world, it's never that simple. Those other vendors were pitching themselves as young, fresh, and new, while we were seen as the reliable, safe and cost-effective choice.

My client wasn't paying a premium to get slow, lousy service. They were buying something else. Your clients are too. Once you figure out what that is, you'll have the secret to building a truly resilient business.

In order to grow my business profitably and stop the commoditization we were experiencing, I would need to realign everything around the things our customers were willing to pay a premium for. Doing so meant letting go of everything I thought I knew so that I could see my industry with fresh eyes. Step one was to rediscover my customer.

Make Customer Obsession a Habit

When things are changing fast, clarity comes from listening not guessing. Make customer obsession a habit and you reduce your risk of being taken by surprise as your market shifts.

Your customers are adjusting at the same time as you are. To stay relevant, you need to meet them where they are now, not where they used to be. And definitely not where *you think they should be*. Listen for signs that their needs are changing.

The simplest things are usually among the most difficult to do well. That's certainly the case with customer obsession. You will find that everyone on your team has an opinion. Very often, those opinions are rooted in the individual's personal experience and bias more than the reality of the situation you are facing.

Your goal is to put the customer's personal experience and bias above those of everyone else. You will put your customer in the driver's seat, continually adapting and reinventing your offers to meet them where they're at and where they're headed at the same time.

Done well, customer obsession will give you the organizational alignment you need when it comes to:

1. Who your ideal customer really is.
2. What they need and how they will move through their relationship with you.
3. How to change workflows to remove friction from the experience of working with you.
4. What to say to engage them across all stages of the customer lifecycle.

The Four Stages of Customer Obsession

In order to do this, you will lead your team through four critical stages of reconnecting with your market.

Those stages are customer discovery, market discovery, opportunity evaluation, and decision.

During customer discovery, you will gather customer feedback to identify emerging pain points and patterns of note that are validated by your data.

In market discovery, you'll evaluate trends in behavior, attitudes, activities, and investment to surface the patterns that are most economically promising or likely to endure.

By now you'll have an abundance of information but very little connection between that information and your business. Opportunity evaluation narrows your focus to the opportunities you are uniquely qualified to pursue.

The final stage is simple. Make a decision and get to work. Let's examine each piece in more detail.

Customer Discovery: Gather Customer Feedback

You can do this in a variety of ways, and I encourage using as many of these channels as you have access to, in order to gather as broad and comprehensive a data set as possible. Focus exclusively on capturing as much feedback as you possibly can. If something doesn't make sense based on your experiences or research, invite your customers to provide more detail and expand on their thinking.

For small business leaders, your best approach is to meet individually with key customers several times a year — not to sell them something but to listen to what's going on in their world, understand what their challenges are, and get a feel for how their needs and wants might be shifting. As you are working through these conversations, try to keep an open mind and avoid jumping to conclusions based on one or two pieces of feedback. The biggest mistake you can make during this stage is falling into the trap of subconsciously listening for feedback that confirms your assumptions while ignoring feedback that challenges them.

One good way to avoid this trap is to engage with a neutral third party, like a research firm or trusted advisor, to have these direct conversations on your behalf. Depending on the size and scale of your business, you may benefit from a variety of additional touchpoints that range from a simple NPS score run from your own CRM to a formal customer survey, or even having an external firm conduct customer satisfaction interviews on your behalf on an annual basis.

However you choose to tackle this step, the process should take no more than a couple of weeks. Things are changing rapidly and you need to move quickly to regain traction.

Analyze Your Data

Now that you have gathered in-depth customer feedback, it's time to bring it all together and identify the patterns that are emerging. You are looking for insights into:

- **The stories lurking behind the numbers:** Find out where clients got stuck, what frustrated them about working with you, what they loved, and why they did (or didn't) refer you.

- **Next look at patterns.** What commonly happens right before your clients leave? What do your best clients have in common? Are there common triggers that show up right before a new client starts looking for help? Are there recurring signs that foreshadow a prospect choosing a competitor?

If you've engaged an advisor to help you with this step, they will likely do most of the heavy lifting here and present you with a summary of their findings as a starting point for your discussions. If you are doing this in-house, these three key areas are where you will find clues to the opportunities before you.

Listen For Emerging Pain Points

Chaos and disruption changes how customers perceive their own needs. Something once considered useless may suddenly become a necessity.

A service they would never have considered allocating budget to may suddenly be in high demand. Or a product they couldn't live without becomes irrelevant overnight.

Listen for signs of adjacent revenue streams, untapped customer groups, and unrecognized risks that weren't on your radar. You'll find these in problems customers are repeatedly sharing, or new challenges affecting a broad segment of their industry. How have their goals and priorities changed? What's different about the way they are making buying decisions?

Look at What's Breaking Down

Cracks will inevitably appear when any business is forced to adapt to an external influence they hadn't planned for. Supply chains fail to keep up or no longer fit the reality of the environment. Customer service suffers as cuts impact the workforce. Marketing messages and sales scripts stop working. Key players might exit the market, seeding doubt in the industry.

Cracks sometimes come from good news too. A surge in demand pulls resources away from key projects as everyone scrambles to keep up with volume. Cash flow may be strained and budget diverted to building needed inventory. Higher volume might require new approaches to automation or increased skills that the team hasn't yet developed.

As you are noticing these patterns of breakdown, think "Where can we step in to help?"

Market Discovery: Follow the Money

The real magic trick is aligning your business to where the money is still flowing. Because not all industries suffer equally during a crisis, you might be able to shift your sales focus to serve customers in an area that's less impacted. Possibly even to one that's reaping the benefits of the chaos moment. Which industries seem unphased by the latest chaos?

Even within impacted industries, not everyone suffers equally. Is there a subset of your existing market that is approaching things differently, investing where others pull back or innovating in ways that increase your value rather than diminish it? Are there specific clusters that are able to meet the challenge head on? They may not be facing the same trade-offs as less well-positioned segments of your market.

Pay close attention to any government stimulus programs, including grants, subsidies, and allowances that could offset the cost of working with you.

Sometimes during this work, you'll find a chrysalis —— a market that is almost but not quite ready to emerge and will grow rapidly once it does. When you're in firefighting mode, it's easy to dismiss these opportunities as too long-term to be viable. You're right in the moment, but only in this moment. Make note of each one that you uncover. You will come back to this list in Act III.

HOT TIP: The rise of GenAI has put immense research power in the hands of anyone with access to an LLM. These tools offer an invaluable assist to your market discovery efforts, but they have significant limitations and should never be your only source. Where budget allows, I encourage my clients to engage a partner skilled in market research. Their trained eye will surface patterns and indicators most business people will miss.

Opportunity Evaluation: Understand What It All Means

It's time to pull your team together and figure out what everything you have learned actually means for your business. Put everything on the table: what you heard, where the pain is, what trends have emerged, and where the money is flowing. Then come to an agreement on which trends and needs are opportunities, which are threats, and which you can safely ignore.

It will be highly valuable to have an outside facilitator or advisor take the lead in these meetings. Their presence allows you to participate fully in the conversation without being distracted. Your facilitator is responsible for ensuring that everyone is heard and all viewpoints are considered. They are also responsible for monitoring the mood and energy of the room, and keeping everyone on time. That said, there is nothing to prevent you from running the process entirely in-house if that's your preference.

Whichever way you approach this brainstorming session, there is one important caveat. For this to work, *everyone* must set aside their personal agendas and consider all the options before you through your customers' eyes. That includes you, dear reader. You are finished when you can confidently complete each of the direction statements below about your most valuable customers.

Decision: Pick a Direction

This step is both the simplest and the most difficult. You are likely to arrive at this point with multiple viable options ahead of you and many different opinions about what to do and in which order. At the end of the day, this is your business and you alone must live with the consequences. In the absence of a clear consensus, once everyone has been heard, you must decide which direction to take.

There are many valid decision-models you can choose from to forge consensus. Your meeting facilitator or advisor will typically lead you through a process that has worked well for them with other teams. In reality, how you get there is unimportant. What matters is that you reach a consensus and agree on your priorities as a team moving forward. Begin by aligning around a single, viable target market. Agree on:

1. The industry in which your ideal customer now operates.
2. The tangible characteristics that they are likely to have in common. Use as many of the following as apply: years in

business, revenue range, number of employees, ownership structure, region in which they operate.

3. Any other tangible characteristics or requirements that apply to your specific business or industry. For example, you might only work with companies who use a specific software or piece of machinery.

At this stage, avoid complicating your target market with vague characteristics like "growth mindset" or "proactive". While valuable during the sales process, these characteristics are typically useless as a targeting mechanism. We will come back to them later.

Next, identify the most lucrative opportunities you have identified within this target market. Ideally, you will come to a ranked list of no more than 3 opportunities that you will pursue. For most small businesses, your chances of success will be greatest if you choose one opportunity to focus on — the one where you believe your organization has the strongest potential to win the category.

Once you have chosen the opportunity to pursue, identify the short, medium, and long-term goals that you must reach to achieve your overall objective. You'll find an exercise guide to help you with this step in the online resource library mentioned throughout this book.

Craft Your Statement of Opportunity

When I'm working one-on-one with clients, we use these insights to develop the foundation for their strategic response plans. They inform the rest of the planning process. Take a moment now to revisit your notes from the exercises throughout this section, then answer these five questions.

1. What is changing in the world around us?
2. How is that impacting the markets we serve and the way our clients prioritize the value we currently offer?

3. What new challenges are our customers experiencing as a result of these changes?

4. What do we need to change about our business to stay relevant and valuable?

5. How will this impact our team; Emotionally, Psychologically, Behaviorally?

Once you've documented your answers, write your statement of opportunity using the template below. If you don't have all the answers quite yet, don't worry. Just fill in the blanks that you can, and highlight the areas where you need more information. Any gaps will become clearer as you work through the next few chapters. You can also scan the QR code at the front of this book to access the companion resources for Act I.

STATEMENT OF OPPORTUNITY TEMPLATE

Our best fit clients tend to operate in [industry]. They are typically [list all known tangible characteristics].

Because of [what's happening], our customers are finding [what's changing for them] and their priorities have shifted to [most important issue], [2nd main challenge], and [3rd main challenge]. As a result, we are experiencing [impact on your business].

However, we have an opportunity to [benefit to your business of making a change] by [action/offer you have identified]. This will serve our customers by meeting their need for [why customers should/will care].

In order to be successful in our efforts, we will need to ensure that our team is equipped to [what you need to change], and to manage the impact of [how your team will be impacted] by [how you will manage the impact of the crisis and the coming change on your team].

6

RETHINK YOUR POSITIONING

By now, you've begun to develop a clearer picture of what's actually driving the chaos you're experiencing, how it's impacting your team, your customers and their buying behaviors, and what opportunities it is creating for your business. You've crafted an opportunity statement that identifies those opportunities and begins to bring clarity to what that means for your organization.

The next step is to operationalize this new insight by crafting a strategic foundation to drive your success. I call this foundation your Growth Architecture Blueprint, and it requires articulating:

- **Your Landscape:** the environment in which you operate, and how you show up in that environment.
- **Your Community:** the broader community of customers you are best suited to serving.
- **Your Ecosystem:** the team, tools, and touchpoints you need to capitalize on your statement of opportunity.

Your Growth Architecture Blueprint

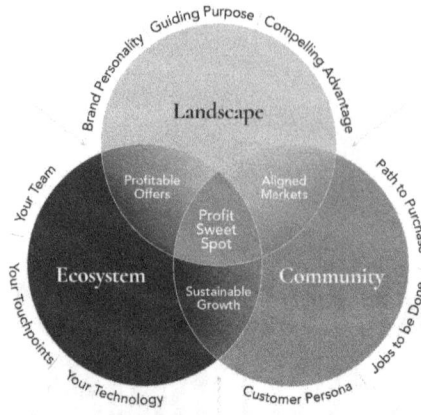

Strategy Before Tactics

When Mark came to me for help with his marketing, he had a laundry list of things he was doing. And an equally long list of campaigns he wanted to roll out. He'd hired agency after agency, each of whom gave him a new spin on the same old recipe. But everything failed to deliver. He admitted that every time there was a leadership change inside a key client account, he had to justify their contract because the incoming manager didn't believe they could fulfil.

It didn't take long to figure out that the recipe wasn't wrong. It was simply incoherent. His positioning was confusing his prospects and killing his pipeline in the process. Instead of creating a brand reputation, Mark was creating noise. Mark's agency partners had been selling him tactics that they could monetize — start an email program, do social media, do paid ads — when what he really needed was a core business strategy against which to evaluate each of those tactics to decide if the juice was worth the squeeze.

As soon as we got Mark's team telling a cohesive story across all customer touchpoints and presenting a consistent image to the world, momentum started to build. He was invited to bid on larger projects with marquis clients and the average value of consulting engagements increased. Best of all? There were no more calls to defend his contract every time a client had a change in leadership.

In this chapter, I'm going to walk you through the process I used with Mark's team to define their Landscape, zero in on the Community that most needed and wanted his help, and map out the Ecosystem he would need to capitalize on the opportunities before him. Let's dig in!

Step One: Define Your Landscape

Most of us start our businesses with the goals of increasing our personal wealth, establishing financial security for our families, and gaining some level of personal freedom. Few of us ever stop to consider the bigger question: *why this business, in this industry , serving these clients?*

That's a mistake. The answers to these questions are the key to uncovering your compelling competitive advantage, the reason prospects should choose your business over everyone else. In the Growth Architecture Framework, we use these questions to help define your Landscape. It is literally the environment in which you have chosen to operate and it is composed of three parts:

- **Your Brand Personality:** how your business shows up in the world.
- **Your Guiding Purpose:** the contribution that you hope to make to your community.
- **Your Compelling Competitive Advantage:** the unique blend of characteristics that sets you apart from competitors.

Together these three elements will articulate everything that makes your business valuable to your most aligned customer — the customer whose preferred way of working is perfectly aligned with your strengths as an organization.

Cautionary note: This isn't about crafting some aspirational, lofty statement that doesn't match the reality of who you are. It's about getting real with yourself and your team, owning how you truly operate as a business. Only by making peace with how your company authentically shows up in the world, can you eliminate the pressure of obsessively monitoring your competitors and trying to keep up with their latest marketing gimmick or discount offer. Instead, you will focus on being the best possible version of yourself. In the process, you'll create a market position that can't be duplicated.

Your Brand Personality

This is a term to describe the way your company engages with others. It's what marketing agencies are focused on when they speak to your brand identify, and it informs both how customers expect your people to behave when they interact with them and the specific kinds of customers that will be drawn to choose you over everyone else.

Your brand personality describes how you interact with your customers, with your teammates, and with your vendors. It should provide context for the way you think about and solve problems, and how you want your customers to feel when they interact with you. Your goal is to craft a concise statement that includes at least two and not more than five adjectives that resonate with you and fits the culture of the business you have built.

You need more than a stylish logo and some favorite colors. Your brand personality defines the work you will excel at, and suggests places that aren't a good fit for your team. Imagine a children's toy maker choosing a serious, analytical product design consultant who never cracks a smile. Or an investment bank targeting high net worth individuals that hires an agency known for fun, playful creative to launch their new venture fund for stuffy, old-money types? How likely is it those initiatives will succeed?

For years, I struggled to position my agency as highly innovative and creative. I hired brilliant designers and copywriters, and we came up with some outstanding campaigns. But that positioning never gained traction. Clients kept telling us they valued my strategic insight. They kept calling us to help them figure out next steps, then hiring someone else more 'creative' to execute those next steps. It took me years to recognize that I was giving away the one thing that clients were most willing to pay for – my own strategic acumen. They saw me as the architect not the interior designer, and fighting that truth was holding my agency back. I never said I was the brightest bulb on the string!

Things turned around quickly when I began to highlight our ability to deliver a road map that would inform everything else you had to do. Our agency went from service bureaux to strategic partner. The decisions we helped clients make impacted not just our work, but also set the direction for how they worked with other vendors. We were writing the playbook, not executing it.

When I engage private clients, we work through a series of exercises to surface the stories and experiences that define their Landscape, crafting a compelling brand personality statement that focuses attention on 2 or 3 descriptive phrases. One of those is to choose at least 3, and no more than 5, adjectives that best describe your company culture. Are you fun and lighthearted? Optimistic and energetic? Serious and analytical? Innovative and business minded? You'll find clues in the words your clients have used to describe your work or their experience working with you.

Don't overthink this. Right now the focus is all on your business and the more honest and authentic you are, the more powerful your positioning statement will ultimately be.

Here's another simple exercise to get you started. Think about your company as though it is a friend you are setting up on a blind date with a colleague. How would you describe them? Grab your workbook and take ten minutes to write down that description in a way that will convince your friend to agree to the date, without exaggerating any characteristics or including any details that aren't 100% true all of the time. Go on, I'll wait...

Got it? Good, now circle all the adjectives you've used in your description. Count how many times you used each one and list them on a separate piece of paper, with the most used adjectives at the top of the list. What are the first 3 words on your list? What themes emerge? If you have a business partner, or key team members, ask them to do the same exercise and then compare notes. The terms that show up across multiple people's lists are very likely the strongest components of your brand personality. Pick the strongest 3 insert them into this brand personality statement.

OUR BRAND PERSONALITY

We are [your company name].

We are [adjective], [adjective], & [adjective].

Your Guiding Purpose

Simply put, your guiding purpose is the contribution you are committed to making to your community. It combines your mission (what you do) with the impact you will have in the world when you are successful in that mission. Who do you want to impact positively, and why?

For example, our guiding purpose at 33Dolphins Growth Strategy is to strengthen local economies by empowering small and medium sized businesses to thrive. Our mission is helping entrepreneurs build sustainable, scalable businesses that enjoy steady, profitable growth. The reason we do it is because I believe that healthy communities only exist when small and medium-sized businesses are thriving.

SME's are the backbone of economic resilience. You provide employment that sustains families. You are more likely to be active supporters of the communities in which you operate and you view your employees as more than a number on a financial spreadsheet. You give youth a dream to aspire to. You add colour, culture, and compassion into our lives.

When we help a company like yours achieve sustainable traction, we're not just ticking a box. We recognize what that means for the people and communities who depend on your business for their livelihoods. It is work we're exceptionally good at and for which we are paid very well, allowing me to reinvest in my business, my team, and my community in the same way.

Now it's your turn. Why did you choose the work that you do? What is the "business friendly" outcome that your work delivers for the people who sign your cheques? Hint: you've very likely got it hanging on a wall poster titled "Vision, mission and values" or something similar. Now take a moment to reflect on what it means when you achieve that mission. Who benefits?

Don't give in to the pressure of having some grand purpose that changes the world. It won't inspire you. Think closer to home. When I started my business, my guiding purpose was very different than it is today. Back then, I had a toddler and a baby on the way. My sole guiding purpose was to build a business that sustained a good life for my family, allowing me to provide for my children while also offering me the freedom to be the kind of mom I wanted to be. Every decision I made hinged on maintaining the balance between those two things. It was only when they entered high-school that I began to feel the pull of a bigger calling. That pull triggered the opportunity for me to rethink my business, ultimately leading me away from agency services back to the intersection of strategic planning and digital reinvention where this book lives.

I'll give you one more example, a large format printing company in my hometown. They'd been operating for over three decades, and employed around 35 people. They took great pride in their work (it really was exceptional) and there were employees who'd been with the company since their first year in business. When the owner of that business talked about the possibility of layoffs or work reductions, it brought tears to his eyes. He didn't need or want more money. He could easily sell the business and retire quite comfortably. His guiding purpose, the fuel that pulled him through the hard times, was his commitment to providing good, well-paying jobs to people he cared about. When he eventually did retire and sell the business, he found a buyer who was aligned around that commitment and many of those employees still work there today.

Did you notice the thing that both my experience and my client's experience have in common? Your guiding purpose statement expresses a strongly held personal belief in the context of delivering a good or service that provides profit to your business. As you craft your guiding purpose statement, remember that purpose without profit is charity, not business.

If you're stuck, reflect on the impact your success has on those around you. How does your business impact your family, your employees, your clients, their families, their employees, their clients. What is it about that impact that lights you up and makes you sit a little taller in your seat? That's your guiding purpose. Be sure you include all three parts: the mission, the business reason, and the broader impact.

- Mission and impact without a business reason is volunteer work.
- Mission and business reason without impact is a commodity.
- Business reason and impact without a mission is an ideal, not a business.

When you're ready to go, grab a pen and paper and complete these statements:

OUR GUIDING PURPOSE

Our Mission

[Company Name] is a [what you are] that [what you do/sell] for [your target market].

Business Reason

We help [clients] achieve [business reason].

Our Impact

When we are successful, [impact] happens because we believe [the reason your impact matters to your community].

Your Compelling Advantage

The final piece of the Landscape puzzle is articulating how your work impacts your clients and how the experience of working with you is different than working with your competitors. We call this your compelling competitive advantage and it's crucial to understand. Your best clients, the ones that are both profitable and that you love working with, will naturally gravitate towards exactly the experience you are best suited to delivering.

Get this wrong and you risk attracting the wrong clients — clients who want what you do but don't value the way you do it. They are likely to leave you faster and, even when they don't, they will be less profitable.

Your first step is to gather all of the customer feedback you gathered during your work on Customer Obsession, both good and bad. If you're still not clear, book a few intentional calls with past customers. Interview them about their experience working with you. What did they appreciate? What wasn't what they expected? What could you have done better? What should you not have done at all? What did you do that no one else in your industry has ever done for them?

Now revisit everything and look for patterns that emerge. Make note of phrases and themes that come up again and again. What do they praise? What do they complain about?

When I'm working one-on-one with a leader and their team, I use insights from this step to guide them through a structured series of exercises designed to give life to their compelling competitive advantage. If you can, I encourage you to also get help as you work through this process. It's incredibly difficult to look at your own business objectively, and often the things about you that make you unique and special are also things you take for granted. You just assume everyone else is also doing them. They're things you don't think are important, or different, or special because you've never experienced what it's like when they are missing. It's hard to see the whole picture while you're inside the painting.

If working with an external advisor isn't possible, and you're still not convinced that you've nailed your secret sauce, try this exercise. Record a video of yourself talking to a friend about your three favorite client experiences. Go into detail about what you did for them, the process you followed, the specific outcomes you were excited about, and the specific outcomes they were excited about. Then review the transcripts of that recording and look for those moments when your face lights up and your energy lifts. What excites you about this aspect of that story? Look for common threads that connect directly back to the nuggets you received from clients in your 360 reviews.

Finally, you will need to write out your compelling competitive advantage using the following format:

OUR COMPELLING COMPETITIVE ADVANTAGE

We deliver [praise you've received about what customers appreciate about you] by [the tangible things you do that deliver that result for your clients].

Be Part of a Community

There's an old but true cliche that "birds of a feather flock together". People with similar characteristics tend to be drawn to similar activities or jobs, and human beings are most comfortable when their day-to-day interactions are with others who share their ideals, work styles, and values. This is good news for you as an entrepreneur because it's going to help you shape your revenue engine to appeal specifically to the exact people most likely to buy from you.

Good things happen when you not only understand the individuals who own the final decision on whether or not to work with you, but you design your systems around meeting their specific needs. Your customers are happy and churn is reduced. You remove friction from the sales process. Your messaging lands with the right people, improving the quality of your leads. You find yourself in more rooms with people who have potential to become your customers.

Developing your Community profile is a powerful tool that enables you to take everything you discovered in Customer Obsession and operationalize it for your business. To do that, you need clarity about:

- **The Buyer Personas** of the people involved in a decision to buy from you.

- **Their Path to Purchase:** what happens inside the organization when they experience needing what you sell.

- **Their Jobs to be Done:** the personal goals and needs of the people involved.

Together these three elements articulate what makes your business invaluable to your most aligned customer. Start by pulling out your Statement of Opportunity from the chapter on customer obsession. Keep it front and center as you work through the three elements of your Community profile.

Your Buyer Personas

Your buyer personas are detailed profiles of the individuals who are involved in the decision to buy (or not buy) what you are selling. Sometimes called customer avatars, they're the tool most favored by branding and marketing agencies to inform creative decisions.

Think of the people working at your best accounts. Note their level of seniority, job title(s), likely educational background, and any other common characteristics you can identify. Your goal here is to understand the whole person beyond the job title. Do they generally have a certain level of experience in their role, or fall inside a typical age range? Are there common lifestyle choices, media consumption habits, and even personality traits found in people who are drawn to this type of work? How do they make decisions? What are their informational needs?

Next, list everyone else in the organization who influences the decision to buy or not buy from you. This might include end users of your product, a financial decision maker, or even a spouse or external advisor. These are the individuals who will either become your champions during the sale or the sceptics who cast doubt on your value. You want to know as much about them as you can, so that you are able to meet their needs during the sales process. Together, these profiles form the buyer personas in your Community profile.

Their Path to Purchase

Every B2B sales transaction must serve the needs of two different stakeholder groups. The first buying group is the organization itself. The business has needs, constraints, and internal politics that must be served. If you fail to meet these, there will be no sale. It's crucial to understand the events that happen inside the business before, during, and after their journey to becoming your happy customer. This is the organization's Path to Purchase.

Start by asking "What usually happens that surfaces the problem(s) we solve?" You're looking for a trigger event, something that makes it urgent for the problem be solved sooner than later. This is the inflection point when your next customer moves from becoming a passive consumer of information to actively in-market for the things you sell. You may end up with a list of these trigger events. If you do, focus only on the 3 most common in the companies who actually buy from you.

Now for each trigger event, map out what people are doing, thinking, saying, and feeling:

- Before the problem even exists.
- When the problem exists, but hasn't yet been recognized.
- When the problem is known, but isn't yet urgent to solve.
- When the trigger event occurs.
- When they try to solve the problem internally.
- When they realize they need external help or resources.
- When they are looking for possible suppliers.

- When they have shortlisted and are engaging with possible suppliers.
- When they make the decision to move forward with someone (or to do nothing).
- When they start working with you.
- When the problem is solved.
- What is the impact to the organization of having this problem solved?

This organizational roadmap forms the "Path to Purchase" that your customer follows, and it will reveal opportunities for you to reach them sooner and more effectively.

Their Jobs to Be Done

The second group is made up of the individual personalities involved in the buying decision. The truth is, their personal agenda isn't always aligned with those of the organization. You can meet all the organizational criteria, have the best price, and still lose the deal to someone who better serves these very personal needs.

For each of your buyer personas, ask these questions: How does the problem we solve impact them personally? Why is it important to solve? What happens if it isn't solved?

In our live workshops, we use the five why's exercise to uncover the deeper needs of your key stakeholders. For my client Devon, when we worked through this exercise with his team, he realized that when his clients came to him, their surface need to meet compliance standards was masking a human need related to job security. Stakeholders needed to show they had taken reasonable precautions to avoid negative outcomes. They wanted a vetted expert who could take the heat if things went wrong.

Jobs to be Done were also at play in my story about the client who was paying another supplier higher fees for the same work, despite weaker results. Our competitor was a major international agency. What mattered? The profile boost of working with a well-known name. This provided an element of ground cover. When campaigns failed, senior leadership were less likely to hold the internal team accountable because the brand name of the supplier carried authority. It was the old "no one ever got fired for hiring IBM" effect. As an added bonus, the big agency relationship opened doors for key members of the client's team. They appreciated perks like invitations to insider events where they might connect with "movers & shakers", potentially opening the door to their next role or promotion. We couldn't compete with that. Fair? No. Reality? Yes.

Once you unlock the personal jobs to be done of your ideal customer groups, you will have a powerful tool in your toolbox. You can focus your attention on fighting only those battles you have a reasonable chance of winning, and stop wasting time chasing clients whose real needs aren't aligned with the value you provide.

Bring It Together: Your Most Aligned Customers

At this point, you have all the information you need to identify the subset of your target market most closely aligned with the value that you bring.

- Their brand personality, and the personalities of the people within the organization are compatible with yours.
- Their personal and corporate values are aligned with your guiding purpose.
- Their jobs to be done are fulfilled by your compelling competitive advantage.

These are your most aligned customers. The clients who are most likely to become raving fans and do more and more work with you. This is the group you will focus your messaging on. When you do, you will attract more prospects who feel compelled to work with you, because you are a perfect fit for what they need.

This works best when everything about your customer journey is purpose-designed to meet these customers exactly where they are, across every stage of their buying journey:

- **Design your brand awareness** to engage them even before they're aware of the problems you solve.

- **Design your marketing** efforts to help them identify those problems earlier in their buying journey, positioning your business as a trusted advisor from the beginning.

- **Craft your prospecting efforts** to appeal directly to those who are realizing the need for outside help.

- **Design your sales process** to follow the organization's Path to Purchase, providing resources that tick the boxes of each stakeholder's Jobs to be Done.

- **Design your fulfilment process** to meet both their tangible and emotional needs as you solve their problem, so that you gain a customer for life.

- **Design your offboarding process** to set the stage for future engagements and secure warm introductions to more prospects just like them.

When you are confident you have defined your most aligned customers, it's time to move on to the next stage of the Growth Architecture Framework: realigning your ecosystem so that every process, message, and action inside your business is tailored to profitably serving these customers above all else.

Susan's Story

Susan's corporate training business faced serious challenges when COVID hit in 2020. Even though she quickly pivoted to virtual delivery, contracts were canceled and no new deals were on the horizon. Things looked bleak but Susan had financial reserves to weather the storm.

As we retrenched through customer obsession, it became clear the training Susan provided was more needed than ever. As a leading expert in her field, there was no reason to change her core product. She did need to change her positioning to align with her customers' new reality, training to level up the skills on her team, and to restructure her sales process to match how customers were buying.

As soon as we began implementing these changes, Susan's business rebounded. Within a few months she was profitable and growing. Her rates went up as clients recognized her value, and a new licensing model was launched. Susan's storm had been short-lived.

ALEX'S NEXT STEPS

Alex made the decision to stop reacting and start leading. He embraced the principles of customer obsession to find out what his clients needed most. Several clients admitted that they were still deeply committed to long-term growth, but financial challenges were forcing them to be more cautious about every dollar. One client mentioned how helpful the free training resources on Alex's website had been for their internal team and asked if more content was coming. Another shared that peer firms in a related industry were struggling with similar challenges and could use the kind of training support his company provided.

That nugget sparked an idea. Alex had found a viable market opportunity that they could leverage. After confirming the need with a few other companies, Alex took his insight back to his core team to rethink their positioning and come up with a plan of action. In the next section, we'll see how Alex used his Statement of Opportunity to reignite growth for his firm.

> # ALEX'S STATEMENT OF OPPORTUNITY
>
> *Because of <u>rising inflation</u>, our customers are finding <u>that money is tight and sales are down</u> so their priorities have shifted to <u>cash flow</u>, and <u>doing more work in-house</u>. As a result, we are experiencing <u>contract cancellations, smaller budgets, and fewer opportunities</u>. However, we have an opportunity to <u>cement our role as a trusted partner</u> by <u>helping our clients achieve their goal of doing more in-house through offering fee-based training resources</u>. This will serve our customers by meeting their need(s) to <u>control their marketing budget and improve in-house skills</u>.*
>
> *In order to be successful in our efforts, we will need to ensure that our team is equipped to <u>develop and deliver fee-based training programs,</u> and to manage the impact of <u>less client marketing work</u> by <u>reallocating some staff to a new training division and refocusing our sales team on new business development to fill the gaps.</u>*

(Re)Design Your Ecosystem

Your Landscape and your Community make up 2/3 of your Growth Architecture. They define the market you serve, how you show up, and who you are best suited to working with. While they certainly evolve over time, it's rare that they will change dramatically in the course of a year or two. However, it's the third and final component that will turn your vision into an actionable business strategy. That component is your Ecosystem.

It encompasses the team, tools, and touchpoints you will use to bring your vision to life. Unlike the other two elements of your framework, you must update it continuously in order to meet the market where it's at. You will hire new people and say goodbye to others. You will find new partners, adopt new technology, and sunset processes that no longer serve you. As your delivery model evolves, you will adjust the ways in which you connect with customers to remove friction from their experience.

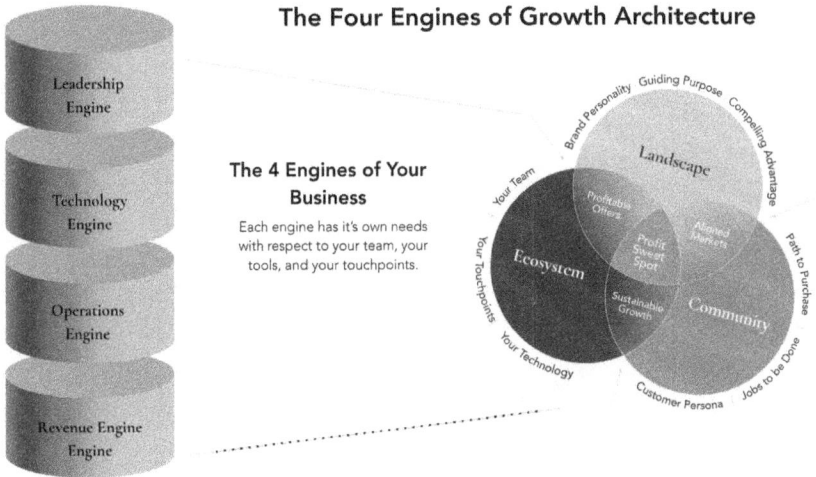

The Four Engines of Growth Architecture

Leadership Engine

Technology Engine

Operations Engine

Revenue Engine Engine

The 4 Engines of Your Business

Each engine has it's own needs with respect to your team, your tools, and your touchpoints.

Brand Personality
Guiding Purpose
Compelling Advantage
Landscape
Your Team
Profitable Offers
Aligned Markets
Profit Sweet Spot
Path to Purchase
Your Touchpoints
Ecosystem
Sustainable Growth
Community
Your Technology
Customer Persona
Jobs to be Done

Your Ecosystem comprises four engines that must operate together for your business to function. They are your revenue engine, your operating engine, your technology engine, and your leadership engine. Each engine has its own needs with respect to the team, tools, and touchpoints necessary to serve your most aligned customers. If any one of these loses its connection to either your Landscape or your Community, your business will falter. So the next step is to realign everyone in your business behind the vision and identity you have just designed. That's exactly what we're going to do together in the next section: Realign.

ACT II: REALIGN

Now is the time to play offense, not defense.

7

THE ROAD AHEAD

It's Monday morning, your first day back in the office after taking some time away to evaluate what's changing and gain some baseline insights into how the current crisis is changing buyer behavior. Now you need to validate those insights with your team, and turn insight into action that measurably drives your business forward in the right direction. Where do you start?

When I'm working live with a client, we hold a series of leadership sessions to craft a "Growth Clarity Blueprint" - a practical, action-oriented roadmap to realign your business with the reality of the market you find yourself operating in. Over the next few chapters, you will do the same for your business.

This is a multi-front war. To win the long game, you will need to make gains across the four critical engines that work together to make your business run.

- **Build a high-impact revenue engine** to stay visible and relevant, with a strong sales pipeline even when times are tough.
- **Optimize your operating engine** to increase your capacity for profitable growth and embed customer obsession into every aspect of your business.

- **Establish a strategic technology engine** to free up your human resources so that you can execute your roadmap without unnecessarily increasing your costs.
- **Strengthen your leadership engine** to ensure your organization continues to adapt, capture opportunities, and sustain growth over time, even when conditions are chaotic.

Accelerate any one of these engines while ignoring the other three and your business will falter. You will go farther and faster by making consistent, gradual improvements across all four engines that keep your business balanced as it grows.

The work you are doing now to develop and execute your Growth Clarity Blueprint is truly the first step in realigning your leadership engine. At the same time, it will empower all levels of your organization to act, catalysing growth while freeing your leadership team to focus on how you can accelerate it.

The next few chapters will guide you to develop your own Growth Clarity Blueprint. You'll define your roadmap and draft your implementation plan, strategically re-deploying resources to make change happen as cost effectively as possible. Finally, you'll discover the common mistakes that could derail your growth so that you can sidestep them.

We'll cover the systems to strengthen your leadership engine in Act III: Reinvent.

8

BUILD A HIGH IMPACT REVENUE ENGINE

If you've been paying attention so far, you're probably wondering "Why revenue engine before operational alignment? Isn't that a fear based approach?" The short answer is no.

Revenue is a *lagging* indicator. It's the harvest at the end of the planting season — it simply tells you how well your revenue engine worked yesterday to deliver the results you're getting today. In other words, your efforts today may not bring money into your business for weeks or months. Sometimes longer.

This time lag between when you start and when your efforts actually deliver net new money into your business is often overlooked. Too many businesses fail simply because they focused exclusively on perfecting their output, waiting too long to crank up customer acquisition. By the time they turn their attention to finding customers, they don't have the financial runway to survive until the harvest.

With that in mind, it's in your best interest to focus first on your revenue engine and then to take advantage of the inevitable time lag to shore up operational alignment so that you are ready to deliver at exactly the same time as your customer is ready to buy.

Your revenue engine encompasses your marketing systems, your sales systems, and your client management systems. Let's start by agreeing on the role each of these plays in driving revenue into your business.

- **Marketing** includes everything you do to be recognized, respected, and preferred by the people with the buying power to do business with you at some future time.

- **Sales** includes all activities designed to engage prospective customers who have the need, the want, *and* the buying power to do business with you <u>right now or in the near future</u>.

- **Client Management** includes anyone in direct contact with customers in the course of delivering your products or services. Generally they hold titles like customer service, customer success, or account management. Their goal is to ensure clients are happy, renew their contracts, and ideally say good things about you to others.

Great Service and Exceptional Products Aren't Enough

Every client I have ever worked with (I literally mean every single one) has answered the question "what makes you different" with some version of "our products are great quality, our service is exceptional, and our value is unmatched." Here's the problem with that approach: Have you ever heard anyone describe their competitive advantage using any of the following statements?

- Our products are pretty lousy. Garbage actually. We're the worst option on the market.

- Our service sucks. Customers complain about it all the time.

- We charge way too much. Our stuff really isn't worth the money we charge for it. I can't understand why anyone even buys it.

If the answer is no, then I submit these things are simply the minimum buy-in to get in the game. They certainly don't differentiate you. Even worse, they perpetuate the myth that if you simply focus on delivering the best value/product/service, you will automatically win. It's a lie.

It's not the best product that matters. It's the product that's marketed the best. Consider the classic business school case study of Beta vs. VHS tapes[13]. Sony's Beta tapes were technically superior, offering better picture quality and more reliable performance. They were also bulkier and more expensive. JVC's alternative, the VHS, was introduced to the market at a lower price point, with a slimmer profile and acceptable quality picture. JVC also allowed other manufacturers to sell VHS players. The resulting competition made VHS much more affordable, and provided consumers with more choice.

VHS won because JVC delivered on customer needs, and did a better job communicating that point of difference. Because there were more VHS players than Beta, studios released new movies on the VHS format, further locking Sony Beta out of the running. Today, you've likely only ever seen a Beta tape if you work in the archives room of a production studio or television station.

Because what's best is always at war with what's already in place, once VHS took the lead, buyer apathy took over. In the market, a solution that's perceived as easiest or good enough will easily beat one that's better but more costly and/or more complex.

Get the Message Right

Have you ever felt like you're doing all the right things and showing up in all the right places, but somehow nothing seems to stick? That's a sure sign that your messaging is missing the mark.

That was the situation my client Jeff found himself in. When we met, Jeff had been investing heavily in marketing agencies and services for over a year. Nothing delivered the promised results. He had a mature business with a strong customer base and an excellent reputation, but their clients didn't see them as the sophisticated service provider that they were.

When I took Jeff through the customer obsession workshop, it was immediately clear where the disconnect was. Jeff's clients were large venues, property management firms, and multi-unit commercial properties like malls and hotels. The operations managers his team interacted with every day appreciated their reliable, efficient service. But they weren't the economic buyer. That buyer was judging them not on personal experience, but on the company's public image.

Jeff's website was woefully out of date and there was no brand consistency between their marketing materials. Their fleet of trucks bore no branding and were frequent targets of graffiti. Jeff's public image gave the impression that his company was a small, mom-and-pop provider. Great for cost effective, quick service. Not such a great option if you were looking for a corporate vendor you wouldn't have to justify to your EVP.

In reality, Jeff had a sizeable staff, a fleet of service vehicles, and a consulting team that delivered exceptional strategic support. Once we aligned the entire company behind a coherent image, branded the fleet of trucks, and updated the messaging to speak directly to the concerns and buying triggers of their economic buyer, Jeff's sales efforts began to see more traction. They were invited to bid on larger and more sophisticated consulting projects, with average project values increasing by over 100%. At the same time, the number of inbound leads grew and the close rate for new opportunities increased.

You can create the same result in your business by answering these questions using the same language that your best customers use in their day to day lives:

- What stories is your most aligned customer telling themselves about the problem you solve?
- What does your most aligned customer need to believe about the problems you solve to be open to a sales conversation?

- What does your most aligned customer need to believe is true to feel confident buying from you?
- What does your most aligned customer need to achieve, personally and corporately, in order for working with you to be considered a success?

The answers to these questions form your magnetic messages. When you communicate them with integrity and authenticity, your most aligned customer will be drawn to you over all other competitors because they will instinctively feel that you understand them better than anyone else. With these messages in hand, it's time to map out your Revenue Engine.

Your Revenue Engine

The way in which your business conducts its sales and marketing activities, your Revenue Engine consists of the team, the tools, and the touchpoints you use to connect with, sell and support the customers who pay your bills.

Your Touchpoints

Your revenue touchpoints are the places and spaces where your organization either connects with, engages, sells, or serves your most aligned clients. Choosing the channels where you will focus your efforts is the first step in designing your Revenue Engine with customer obsession as your guidepost. You will do this by answering the questions below to build a customer journey accountability map. Make sure to download the customer journey template from the resources center to help you organize your insights.

Where do your aligned customers gather? Are there industry associations, online communities, conferences or clubs where they are likely to hang out? Do they use some social media channels more than others? How will you participate in these channels?

Where do your aligned customers get information? What publications do they read, both online and in print? What podcasts do they listen to? What content creators do they follow? Where do they ask questions about the problems you solve? What options are there for you to be present in these channels?

Where do your aligned customers ask for referrals? Who do they trust to recommend products and services? Are there individuals, groups, websites, or platforms outside of their personal networks where they go to find solutions to their problems? What can you do to either partner with or otherwise be visible and known in these channels?

How do your aligned customers prefer to communicate at each stage of their relationship with you? What are the communication methods favored by the buyers inside your aligned customer companies? Do they prefer email? Text? Phone? Slack? WhatsApp? Social media? Something else? Will you try to engage across all of these or choose only the two or three most important ones?

Now that you have these channels listed, map them to each stage of the customer's buying journey. Does the preferred channel change over the course of the customer relationship? How will you accommodate these changes?

Your goal is simple. Communicate the information your customers need at each stage of your relationship in the specific channels where they are most likely to discover it. You now have the framework around which to build your revenue engine.

Your Team

The next step is building your team. Begin by deciding which roles will be accountable for success at each stage of the customer's journey. Is that role on the marketing team? The sales team? The account management team? Will responsibility be shared, and if so, to what degree will each participant be held accountable for results?

Pull out your customer obsession notes and tag each section of your customer journey with the team that will be held accountable for it. If any activity is owned by the fulfilment team, go ahead and label it "Operating Engine". For now, put it aside so that you can focus on the stages owned by marketing, sales, and account management. The stages remaining will typically include some variation of Awareness, Curiosity, Consideration, Conversion, and Retention/Renewal. Note what skills will be needed at each point to build a complete picture of the skills that you will need to have in place on each team.

Use the answers to these questions to map out your ideal organizational chart for each of these teams. What role on your leadership team will lead them? What roles will manage budgets, drive campaign ideas, and oversee the execution of the work? Which roles will manage vendor relationships? What execution skills do you need on your internal team?

Now look at the people you have on those teams today. Include any freelancers or agencies with whom you do regular work. Which ones have the skills and experience listed on your organizational chart? Write the names of the people or partners who currently fill these roles in the boxes on your org chart. Highlight any spots that are left unfilled. These are gaps you will need to address.

When this is finished, pause and take a step back. Are you putting the same individual's name in multiple boxes? If so, which of the boxes are they *best* suited for? Which ones don't really match their skills? Are some people in the wrong box? Would they be better suited to a different role on your team? Are you paying for skills you no longer need? Who needs training to help them progress? Are you outsourcing work that could more economically and effectively be delivered by an in-house staff?

As you answer these questions, you will gain clarity on where the gaps are in your organization so that you can take action to fill them - either through training, restructuring, hiring, or a combination of all three.

Keep in mind as you work through your planning that any time you are working with an outside vendor, your cost per unit of work will be significantly higher than if you were to employ that skillset directly. Unlike an employee, the agency must account for its own operating overhead, marketing and cost of sales in the fees it charges you.

In practical terms, this simply means that your marketing investment will yield fewer outputs, but hopefully those outputs will be of higher quality and greater impact because they are being developed by people with significant expertise and skill. As a general rule, you will be best served by outsourcing the work that is either infrequent or highly specialized, or where you don't have enough need for those skills to justify the expense of a full-time employee.

I have seen some clear patterns emerge when I am working with clients.

- Sales roles and account management roles almost always need to be in-house.
- Outbound lead generation activities like cold emailing & cold calling are often best when supported by external vendors, automations, or a combination of the two.
- Marketing activity coordination is almost always best managed by an in-house coordinator or marketing manager.
- Social media content and engagement is typically most effective and most affordable when it is owned by an in-house staff.
- Most other marketing execution tasks can be delivered by any of an in-house staff, a freelancer or contractor, or an agency.

For many SMEs, leadership roles are most cost-effective with the support of an external advisor. As a general rule, until your business reaches at least $20M ARR, you will achieve a better ROI working with fractional experts in both the CMO and VP Sales roles. Below this threshold, a full-time hire puts you at a disadvantage. You will either hire someone not quite ready for the role in an attempt to balance budget against filling a spot on your org chart or divert too much of your budget to a single role, hampering everyone else's ability to deliver.

Once you have your organization chart established, work out the total salary cost for all internal staff, being sure to account for benefits. Then estimate your investment in any vendors or freelancers that will do recurring work for you and add that to your budget for team.

Depending on the size of your business, it may make sense to separate your budgets for each function - sales, marketing, and account management. However this is a purely operational decision. Do what works best for your current structure and financial situation. There is no value in adding complexity unless it's absolutely needed.

Your Tools

Now it's time to focus on the resources your team will need to execute effectively. The specific tools you need will be dependent on your industry, your revenue plan, and your ability to invest. Your toolset encompasses the systems & processes your team must follow, the technology and equipment they will use, a variety of sales and marketing assets or templates, and anything else that applies to your particular operation.

For most B2B businesses, your technology needs will include a CRM, a marketing automation platform, a website, some type of design software, content creation tools, all supported by some level of automation and AI. You will also benefit from project management tools to help your team keep track of multiple different initiatives. You may need trade show display materials, sales collateral, scripts, canned presentations, promotional items, and rate sheets. There is no magic here - focus on the basics and get those right first.

Make a list of everything you think you will need and do some research to establish the typical investment by successful businesses similar to yours.

Formalize Your Budget

Now that you have your Revenue Engine defined, it's time to figure out what it will cost to implement. Most small and mid-sized B2B companies allocate between 8% and 15% of total revenue on the sales function, with a few industry-specific variations. Marketing investment also falls between 8% to 15% and varies based on both your industry and where you are on your growth path.

If your planned investment falls far outside these ranges, consider why and whether you need to make adjustments. Invest too little and you will set your team, and your business, up for failure. Invest too much and you risk permanently squeezing your margins and impacting your ability to invest in other critical growth areas.

A note on pricing: It's crucial to build allowance for these costs into your pricing model. While a detailed discussion of pricing strategy is beyond the scope of this book, it's worth noting that pricing mistakes are the most common profit-killer in small business. Make sure that the price you charge for your products and services includes *all* the costs you incur to operate your business.

In my experience, most small and mid-sized B2B firms should plan on allocating roughly 15–20% of revenues to sales (team costs, CRM, commissions, salaries) and another 8–15% to marketing. Taken together, that means a healthy revenue engine typically runs 20–35% of gross revenue. The right number for your firm will depend on several factors, including the size of your firm, the market's awareness of your brand, and your specific goals.

Help, My Plan is Unaffordable!

What do you do when the investment needed to implement the plan you have put together makes your brow sweat and your heart skip a beat? Don't despair, it doesn't mean you're trapped.

This is actually a very common scenario. If you've never had these expenses, your pricing very likely hasn't been set to accommodate them. If this is the case, are you able to increase your fees to create some room? Do you have available capital you can allocate to kick-start your growth?

Another common scenario is that marketing and sales function costs have previously been buried in other budgets. Take a look at what you actually spent last year and where those costs were recorded. You may find the gap is smaller than you think.

If you really can't see a path to finding the dollars from your operations to fund marketing, then the next question becomes what investment *is possible*? Can you borrow money or take on an investor?

If none of these are viable options, you can scale back your vision (and your expectations) to fit your budget. It will simply take you longer to gain momentum and reach your goals. What parts of your plan can you get started on right away? What needs to be funded in future from net new revenues?

It's important to recognize your true financial constraints as you complete this final step. If you are unrealistic or dishonest with yourself about your ability to invest in the resources you need, you will find yourself frustrated by a lack of momentum in your revenue engine.

Activate Your Revenue Engine

You've hired the people, provided them with the tools, and clarified the channels that matter. It's now time to let them do the work to make it all happen.

Start by clearly communicating your goals for the business and how their contribution is needed to reach them. Make sure everyone on your team is aligned behind your Growth Clarity Blueprint, setting both team and individual goals for the coming quarter. Then get out of the way. Your focus needs to switch to your Operating Engine, ensuring that every aspect of your customer's experience is consistent with the promises you are making.

However, this doesn't mean you walk away entirely. Keep a close eye on the results you're getting from your investment by checking in with your revenue team regularly. We'll explore the management and oversight systems you can use to embed a culture of accountability into your organization in Act III: Reinvent.

The Exception to the Rule

Most businesses have relatively happy clients when we begin working together. Their operations engine isn't perfect, but it's good enough to get the job done. Every once in a while, that's not the case. When you find yourself struggling with customer churn, an unhealthy level of unpaid invoices, or frequent customer complaints, you may have a critical problem in your operations engine. It's crucial to solve that problem before you turn up the heat on new business. If this is you, I recommend you work through the chapter on operational alignment to stop the bleeding before you activate your revenue engine to reignite your growth.

Ryan's Story: Frictionless Expansion

Ryan and his partner had been successfully running their boutique MSP firm for a few years. They'd acquired some marquis clients and smartly invested early in building out a strong brand and positioning for their firm. However revenue was stagnant and Ryan was continually being dragged into the day to day operations of the organization. Unpredictable margins sometimes meant that Ryan had to forego his own salary to make payroll. A scan of his customers quickly surfaced the key source of friction.

Like most small businesses, Ryan had accepted every new client that came his way. As the business grew, this meant he was supporting a very diverse client community with equally diverse needs and expectations. His team was constantly adjusting processes to fit each client, leading to inefficiency and overservicing. In order to grow effectively, Ryan would need to lean into his most aligned customer and put a stop to customizing processes.

Once we identified the aligned customers in Ryan's existing client base, we were able to design his revenue engine to focus on engaging more companies like them. All that was required? A few simple tweaks to language, messaging, and cadence. No expensive rebrand needed.

Next, we revisited Ryan's pricing model to be sure that his hourly rates were calibrated to account for all the costs that the business incurred and allow for a fair profit margin. With fresh clarity on the minimum hourly rate he could charge and still remain profitable, Ryan was able to establish new and stricter policies around pricing and packaging. His new packages were tailored to the needs and expectations of his most aligned customer, with a pricing model that ensured profitability and stabilized cash flow.

This clarity empowered account managers and sales reps to be more proactive and focused, leading to even stronger client relationships and a growing customer base.

I checked in with him about six months later. Business was thriving. Ryan had now expanded his leadership team to free up his own time and he was in the process of acquiring another firm that would solidify their presence in a new market.

9

ALIGN OPERATIONS TO KEEP THE PROMISE

Operational alignment simply means designing your operating engine to keep the promises your marketing makes. Making sure that your customers have a good experience at every point in their relationship with you is crucial to your business resilience.

When you do this well, it's like turning up the dial on your revenue engine. You benefit from longer relationships with clients who buy more from you and willingly introduce you to more people like them who will be happy to work with you.

Get it wrong on the other hand, and you will struggle to maintain momentum. Trust is eroded, churn rises, and margins shrink. Think about the times when you have been promised one experience and received another. That gap is operational misalignment and it's the silent killer of customer loyalty.

The Hidden Cost of Misalignment

Operational misalignment shows up in one of two ways. Both are dangerous, but they impact your business differently. Fortunately, the clues are hiding in plain sight.

When your operations aren't delivering what your marketing has promised, churn goes up and trust erodes. No matter how good your marketing is, you'll be trapped in a never-ending cycle of replacing lost customers with new ones. It's exhausting and stressful. Over time your enthusiasm for your business will fade along with your confidence.

On the other hand, when you routinely deliver more than you promised, you're actually training your customers to demand more value than they paid for. Instead of earning loyalty, you put your business on the fast track to shrinking margins and strained relationships.

Neither dynamic is sustainable. In both cases, your business suffers. Your customers end up feeling let down and lose trust in your services. Your team feels disrespected, hurting morale and culture. And you? You shoulder the burden of trying to hold it all together, with all the insomnia and resentment that comes with it.

Your Chaos Is A Gift

Whether your chaos comes from an external challenge or from reaching a new level of success, there's nothing like entering unknown territory to shine a spotlight on your flaws. Many successful businesses hit this wall as they approach or cross the million-dollar threshold. It happens again as you move from $5M to $10M. This is the paradox of success. In fact, successfully operating your business means continually navigating this balance as your company and your customers evolve.

When your world shifts unexpectedly, it can feel like all your weaknesses are on display for the world to see:

- Every area you've underinvested in starts to falter.
- Every underperforming team or program suddenly feels urgent.
- Every relationship you felt uneasy about, but didn't have the time or courage to confront, breaks down.

- Every product line, offer, or target market that should have been abandoned becomes a profit vampire.
- Every failed marketing campaign or "sure-thing" prospect who said no feels like a personal rejection.

Faced with these growing pains, it's easy to convince yourself that everything will return to normal if you just tighten up your management style. But gritting your way through choppy waters has a habit of slowly eroding your resilience and limiting your ability to take advantage of juicy opportunities that come your way. In the meantime, you've put a band aid on a gaping wound. The root of the problem is still sitting there, waiting to be exposed at the next bump in the road.

You have an opportunity right now to consciously design all aspects of your Operating Engine - the team, the tools, and the touchpoints - around your most aligned customers' path to purchase and jobs to be done. That's how you build a business that can withstand chaos without sacrificing the heartbeat that drives its success. So where do you begin?

Audit the Customer Experience

This is where customer obsession becomes operational strategy. You've already done the hard work of clarifying who your customer is and what they care about. You activated that knowledge to attract your most valuable customers in your Revenue Engine. To optimize your operations, every internal system and process must also reflect that understanding.

Revisit everything that happen in the process of servicing your clients, engineering the entire customer experience to deliver exactly what was promised. No more. No less. Pull out your Customer Obsession notes and make sure you can answer these three questions about every aspect of your customer experience:

- What did your customer think they were buying? *Tip: this usually isn't what you think you were selling.*

- How do the results they achieve compare to what they thought they were buying?
- What does it actually feel like to work with you?
- Where does the experience deviate from what was promised?

Pay particular attention to the Path to Purchase followed by the organizations where your ideal customers are found. Evaluate the touchpoints that follow the sale: onboarding, communication cadence, project handoffs, response times, reports, and deliverables. What is your company doing at each step along that path? Be as specific as you can. What aligns? What doesn't? What feels frustrating, slow, confusing, or inconsistent?

Next, revisit your ideal customers' "Jobs to be Done" — the personal goals and aspirations of your best customers. Revisit all of the touchpoints that follow the sale again, this time asking if your ideal customer's innate personal needs are being met? If not, what can you change to meet them?

Finally, take a close look at the last 3 to 7 projects you completed. Compare what was actually delivered to what was included in your fees. Are you doing more than you are paid to do? Is the work you are actually doing different from what was scoped? How is this communicated? What were the final outcomes? Did they meet, exceed, or fall short of the outcomes they were promised at the outset of your engagement? Why or why not? Did you promise something you couldn't control? Did you deliver less than you committed to? More?

Even small gaps in any of these three areas are enough to plant seeds of doubt in working with you again. Design every interaction to match your customers' ideal experience as closely as possible.

Optimize Your Team, Tools and Touchpoints

As with your Revenue Engine, your Operating Engine will be constrained by the resources available to execute on your promises. Under-resourced teams are more likely to fall short of client expectations, while over-resourced teams are prone to overdelivering without paying close enough attention to margins. The worst of all scenarios is an under-resourced team operating in a culture where overdelivering is the expected norm. This group is most at risk of not simply missing deadlines, but also making serious mistakes that can ultimately put your entire business at risk.

Let's start with your operations touchpoints.

Your Operating Touchpoints

Your operations touchpoints include the platforms and places where your teams communicate with each other, as well as the spaces and channels where you interact with clients in the course of working with them. Aim to balance between convenience for your clients with viability for your team. Here are a few questions to get you started:

- **How do you keep track of progress?** Do you use project management software? Time tracking tools? Will you invite clients to have any level of access in these channels?

- **How do you onboard new clients?** What is the sequence of bringing a new client into your business? Do you provide educational resources to help them get up and running? Do you hold a kick-off meeting for the project? Is client participation friction free? Is the content delivered to the standard you need? Are there gaps that leave important details unspoken or questions unanswered?

- **How will you handle project specific communications?** How frequently will you connect with clients? Share files and data? What are the communication methods favored by the people inside your aligned customer companies? Do they prefer email? Text? Phone? Slack? WhatsApp? Something else? Do you join a client's Slack channel or agree to use their project management software? Why or why not? How does this decision impact your processes?

- **How do you send invoices and collect payments?** What payment methods do you accept? At what point are you paid for your services? What happens if a payment is late? How do you ensure invoices are accurate? How do you bill for extra work?

With these questions answered, evaluate every touchpoint for unnecessary friction. Where does the way you show up differ from the promises you have made? What needs to change to fix that? You should now have the framework around which to build your Operating Engine.

Your Team

The next step in realigning your Operating Engine is to right size your team. It's time to flesh out the organizational chart for this part of your business. It may be quite similar to the one you have now, or quite different. That really depends on what you discovered during your customer experience audit. Ask the same questions you did before:

- What role(s) will lead this team?
- Who roles will manage budgets, drive campaign ideas, and oversee the execution of the work?
- Which roles will manage vendor relationships?
- What roles do you need to execute deliverables?
- What partners will you need to secure?

Once again, put the names of the people or partners who currently fill these roles into each of boxes. Highlight any boxes currently unfilled and take a step back, asking the same questions here as you did earlier when designing your revenue engine. You can also find them in the workbook resources that accompany this book.

Next, pull out the customer journey accountability map that you created as you designed your revenue engine? Does your refined org chart remove friction from the areas you flagged as "Operating Engine" roles. Are there roles that should be added? Combined? Or removed entirely? Which skills will you need to add or strengthen to full your promises during this portion of your customer's journey?

Now that you have a complete org chart, it's time to make sure you have the right people in every seat. Go through your org chart one more time asking these questions for each person:

- Is this the best use of their skills? If not, where would they be better suited?
- Do they need training or skills development to truly shine in this role?

During the process, you may find that some of the people on your team no longer have a clear place in your business. You may have more people on payroll than you need to fulfill on the volume of business you are delivering, requiring layoffs or cutting full-time jobs back to part-time. Some people may be doing work that no longer supports your strategy, requiring restructuring or job changes. Some jobs may have outgrown the abilities of the people filling them.

This exercise isn't about cutting costs. It's about aligning your workforce to set the foundation for your future growth. When a loyal employee can be redeployed into a more valuable role, do it. If a slowdown is temporary, find a smart way to bridge it without losing both capacity and high-performers. Where you can provide training to help a good employee get to the next level, it's an investment worth making. But if someone is genuinely no longer a fit and you have no place for them, letting them go will help release the cash you need to invest in recovery.

This is the hardest part of achieving operational alignment, having tough conversations with people you care about. As tempting as it might be, don't shy away from them. The longer you allow a point of friction to remain in your business, the more you undermine your own credibility with clients, employees, and even yourself. Take stock and decide whether a performance improvement plan is a workable solution. If it's time to part ways, act quickly with empathy and graciousness to solve the problem.

Once you have your organization chart established, work out the total salary cost for all internal staff being sure to account for benefits. Then estimate your investment in any vendors or freelancers that will do recurring work for you and add that to your budget for team.

Your Operating Tools

Even the best talent will fail at their task if they don't have the resources they need to execute effectively.

The specific tools you need are specific to your business. There is such a broad range of possibilities here that it is impossible to provide a simple list. Consider the physical tools that you use to do the work you do, including everything from machinery to computer hardware. Then add in soft tools like your ERP platform, project management suite, and accounting software. It's very likely that your accountant can pull a pretty comprehensive list of existing tools from your bookkeeping system to save you time and get you started. Remember to make note of any standardized processes that your teams must follow, things like templates, SOPs, playbooks, etc.

As before, take a moment to calculate the costs associated with acquiring these resources so that you can integrate them into your operations budget.

Use Technology to Amplify (Not Replace)

Technology can be a powerful operational tool, but only if you use it to support your people, not sideline them. We'll dig deeper into digital adoption in the next chapter. For now, stay alert for ways to leverage your existing tech stack to give your team back their time and sanity. Just remember that technology won't solve a process problem. It will just speed it up.

Suzy's Story: Eliminate Wasted Effort to Fund Growth

When Suzy completed her operational alignment audit, we realized that client data was scattered across multiple systems. There were no standards for how information was entered, and she alone knew how to wade through the data maze to find it.

Things came to a head when she tried to launch a renewal campaign to past customers who hadn't worked with her in several months. Suzy quickly realized it was impossible to pull a mailing list of those customers that contained accurate, up-to-date information. Her sales rep couldn't even enter the necessary contract dates into the CRM. The fields literally didn't exist.

Every day, her team was wasting hours doing manual workarounds. And that was causing errors throughout the customer experience journey. Fixing it wasn't about working harder. It was about bringing discipline and structure to how client data was handled across all of her systems. Once they did, the entire team became more productive, and the business began to grow.

Budgeting Operations: Revisit Your Pricing

Now that you've got a clear picture of what the ideal client experience *should* look like, it's time to revisit your pricing. Begin by adding up all of the costs you have identified so far in your Operating Engine. For each product or service you sell, work out the actual cost to provide the experience your customer needs. This is the true unit cost of that product or service. Write this number down, you'll need it later.

For our purposes, we're going to keep the pricing discussion very basic.

Is the amount of money you are charging sufficient to cover the unit cost of what you are selling, plus the administrative and operational overhead you incur to deliver it, plus the cost of actually selling it, plus the cost of marketing your business, and still have a respectable percentage left over to create financial resilience and invest in your future?

As a general rule of thumb, as a small to mid-sized B2B services company your unit cost should fall somewhere between 25% and 40% of your total revenue, depending on your industry and the size of your business. This benchmark ensures you have enough money coming all of your business costs with profit left over at the end of year. Remember, profit is where your ability to invest in growth and secure a longer runway happens. It is the key to building a resilient business.

To determine your target price range:

1. Divide your unit cost by 25% to determine the high end price.
2. Divide your unit cost by 40% to determine the low end.
3. Your fees should fall somewhere between these two prices.

If you have access to industry benchmarks or best practices for unit cost as a percentage of total revenue, use those numbers to get a more accurate viable price range.

Charge below the minimum price and you will struggle with profitability. You will also be viewed as a commodity by your market. Where you are too far above the maximum price, you may be vulnerable to losing customers to a strong competitor with a better value story.

Sometimes price increases aren't possible due to market pressures. In this situation, you will need to reduce your operating costs to remain profitable. You might renegotiate with vendors, or rescope the deliverables at your current rates. This is also often where technology enablement helps (we'll talk about that in the next chapter). However you do it, please address this sooner than later. The longer that you continue to sell a product for less than you need to pay your bills and earn some profit, the deeper you will force yourself into financial chaos.

Be sure to build flexibility into your offer structure. Some aspects of what you do will be non-negotiable for every client. Others are pieces clients might give up in order to reduce their total cost, with no loss of experience or satisfaction. Think of the damage insurance offered to you every time you buy an electronic gadget. Some people buy these religiously, others don't see the value. Set your team up for success by ensuring they can adapt in real time to the situation at hand without eroding your profitability.

Finally, choose a date beyond which you will no longer honor your "old" pricing and communicate it clearly to your team. If current clients are affected, you will also need to be sure that the rollout is done with sufficient notice and in accordance with your contracts in order to avoid sticker shock.

Use Cash Flow As an Operational Mirror

It will take investment to kick-start your resilience building journey. Very often, this investment will come out of your cash reserves. Seeing those reserves dwindle is a stressful experience, so it's important to maintain a close eye on the context in which your investments are being made.

Your cash flow from operations is the first place that weak points in your financial management systems show up. If any of these common cash-flow killers are alive and well in your business, make sure you address them before you kick off any major strategic investment initiatives:

- Are you getting paid before you have to pay others?
- Are your invoices being sent promptly and followed up on consistently?
- Are your invoices paid promptly or are you starting to see delays?
- Are you carrying more fixed overhead than your delivery model requires?

These are operational questions, not just financial ones. Review your payment terms, your vendor agreements, and your timing gaps. Clarity here strengthens your resilience and buys you critical runway.

Once your financial house is in order, I recommend establishing a strategic budget for your realignment efforts that is separate from your operating budget. This will make it easier to keep your strategic spending within reason, while also making sure your operations remain profitable. It will also help you make the case for investment should you decide to seek external funding to support your journey.

Your cash flow from operations is a barometer for how well you are doing. If at any time your operating margin *before* strategic expenses dips below break-even, it may be time to slow your progress or take a short pause to allow your revenue volumes to catch up.

Patience is More Than a Virtue

By now, it's likely that you've uncovered a treasure trove of problems and you're eager to fix them. That's good. Just tread carefully. This is where most leaders make their biggest mistakes.

As the business leader, your job is to have the big vision and see the full picture at all times. Your job is also to decide what part of that vision is the highest priority, and give your team the time and space to do the work without overwhelming them with so much change that they can't help but drop the ball. This is a marathon, not a sprint. Take it one step at a time. You'll be amazed at the impact even a small change can make.

I experienced this myself when I decided to pivot my done for you services agency and focus on the consulting and advisory work that I love. I was eager to make the shift but in practice it took more than two years to wind down long-term client relationships and make sure those clients were well taken care of. It also took time to right-size my team, maintaining a careful balance between properly resourcing our legacy agency services while shifting incoming business to purely strategy and consulting engagements. Ultimately, the shift was gradual and smooth, allowing me to maintain positive relationships with both the staff and the clients who were leaving. Patience kept the door open for future opportunities to work together.

This is one of the many parts of your journey where an external advisor can be invaluable. They're not emotionally tied to your systems or assumptions, and they can help you see things you've grown blind to.

Key Takeaway: Delivery is the Root of Trust and Resilience

Customer obsession isn't just a mindset, it's a design spec. True operational alignment means that you:

- Keep your promises to customers.
- Respect the value you bring to your clients.
- Reinforce trust in all relationships, both internal and external.
- Free your most valuable resources to invest in growth.

Your Turn

It's common to feel like you have a lot of work to do and wonder how you're going to find the time. Overwhelm is the biggest killer of momentum that small and mid-sized business leaders face. So this is your reminder that you can do it all, just not all at once.

It's important to prioritize the changes you are making, so that the things that will have the biggest impact on your customer experience are tackled first. Begin by asking yourself which part of your delivery is so misaligned with your promise that it is actively sowing distrust. What if realigning that single piece with your promise is your greatest growth lever?

My client Paul had a strong business and exceptional customer loyalty scores. When we surveyed his clients, they all complained of only one point of friction. Invoices took too long to arrive once the job was done. This delay caused problems with their own invoicing processes and resulted in cash flow issues in their businesses. Simply speeding up the frequency with which invoices were generated solved this problem and removed a major point of friction from the customer journey.

Rather than trying to solve everything at once, try this:

- Choose one area to focus on.
- Audit one delivery touchpoint in that area this week.
- Identify a friction point that erodes trust.
- Assign someone accountability for fixing it.
- Assign yourself the task of following up to be sure progress is happening.

Once momentum starts building on the first touchpoint, move on to the next one and repeat the process. If your company is large enough that you have a management team around you, then I encourage you to delegate the bulk of this work to them.

Not only will your progress be faster, the drag on your time will be significantly reduced. Your role becomes that of the conductor. You will work with each of them to maintain a steady pace of change that delivers positive impact without disrupting your ability to deliver on your customer promises.

10

LEVERAGE TECHNOLOGY FOR EFFECTIVENESS AND INNOVATION

Now that both your revenue and operations are moving in the right direction, the solution to the inevitable bottlenecks or stumbling blocks you encounter will often be found in your tech stack. In this chapter, we're going to go deep on the technology that powers your business so that you shift from using technology as a tool to leveraging it as a strategic amplifier in your business.

Whether you own a restaurant or SaaS company, one truth is ubiquitous in modern times. There is no such thing as a business strategy that doesn't include some level of digital adoption planning. Running your business without technology is like racing NASCAR on a pedal bike and expecting to win. It's a fool's errand.

And you? You're no fool.

In this chapter, you will define your technology engine. You will discover the four styles of leaders when it comes to digital adoption. You'll learn which problems technology is best at solving, as well as the ones it doesn't handle well at all. We'll also address the pace of change, and how successful leaders balance caution with proactivity.

By the time we're finished, you'll have something much more powerful than a list of tools. You'll have a framework for making smarter, faster, and more human decisions about digital transformation and a vision for how your organization can leverage technology for lasting competitive advantage.

The Four Styles of Tech-Adopting Leaders

When it comes to technology, I've encountered four styles of leadership. What's most interesting is that all business leaders take on different styles at different times, depending on the situation and their needs. In fact, if you've led a business for any length of time, you've likely worn each of these hats at some point. I know I have.

None of the four styles is inherently wrong. Each brings both benefits and risks for your business. The only thing that matters is recognizing which style you're currently operating from, and taking conscious steps to counteract the risks that mode introduces into your decision-making process.

As you read through each style, try to remember a time when you were thinking or acting from this mental mode. What was happening in your business or your life that was prompting your attitudes? By recognizing these triggers, you'll be better equipped to test your own thinking when confronting a new technology.

The Blind Adopter

The Blind Adopter jumps into every technology trend, often without a clear problem to solve or a plan to measure results. Blind adopters absolutely love innovation. If we're honest, maybe they just love new. This technology style thrives on being first. They've had CRMs since most of us were still wrangling with Rolodexes. They brag about their AI assistants and their phone is brand new. This style is motivated by two conflicting emotions: ambition and anxiety.

- **Ambition is hunger for opportunity.** It drives desire to stay ahead and willingness to risk the unknown in search of a big payoff. It positions you to take advantage of founder discounts and lifetime deals, which can dramatically lower costs. Ambition can lead to huge wins and early market gains for the few who manage to avoid the downside of Ambition's twin brother, Anxiety.

- **Anxiety delivers constant fear** that you're already falling behind. That you've missed the opportunity by acting too slowly. It pushes you to leap without a clear strategy, taking over-hyped promises at face value without pausing long enough to assess the downside. Anxiety keeps you in a state of constant tech switching, without ever realizing the potential ROI of your investment.

Blind adopters don't lack courage. They lack a filter.

Are you in Blind Adopter mode? Before rushing full-steam ahead with the next shiny object, consider "Are we solving a pressing business challenge or simply chasing the feeling of progress with no clear destination in mind?"

The Pragmatic Adopter

The Pragmatic Adopter carefully evaluates every new technology before they execute. They read all the tech blogs, watch the webinars, attend the conferences. Their best friends are Blind Adopters. Equally technology curious and open-minded, they wait to adopt new systems until there is a strong business reason to do so. They may have jumped on past trends too quickly and have the scars to prove it. Or they've seen their friends and colleagues crash and burn when new turned into nasty.

These leaders are still early movers, they're just not first movers. They act quickly enough to gain advantage, carefully enough not to burn cycles. They think in terms of fit: *Does this align with our priorities? Do we have the bandwidth to implement and adopt it well? What do we actually lose if we put this off until...?*

This style is the most balanced of the four, combining proactivity and enthusiasm with the measured decision making of the strategist. It often leads to the most successful digital adoption initiatives, the ones that drive both efficiency and innovation without burning out the team. But this style also has its downside.

When that carefully constructed patina of pragmatism is masking an underlying fear, this mode can lead the Pragmatic Adopter to a state of paralysis where decisions get stalled waiting for the stars to align perfectly.

Are you in Pragmatic Adopter mode? When you catch yourself asking for yet another business case, or looking for reasons this idea might not work, stop and consider "What's the smallest viable way to test this idea with real users?"

The FOMO Adopter

FOMO adopters are among the last to embrace new technologies. They don't allow themselves to fall too far behind the crowd, but they follow rather than lead. FOMO Adopters prefer to wait until the writing is on the wall. Once they've heard "You're not using [X]?" from a competitor one too many times, they scramble. When they do finally invest, they are often forced to overspend because urgency leaves little room for thoughtful negotiation or internal preparation.

FOMO Adopters are often the most battle-scarred and change-fatigued leaders. They're tired of learning, and then re-learning, and then re-learning again. Their advantage is that they rarely get burned by new technology that causes more pain that it's worth. By the time they move, most of the bumps in the adoption process have already been smoothed out. The platforms are mature and generally quite stable. That's the benefit.

The risk isn't in *what* they buy, but in *how* they implement. All those hasty rollouts without adequate time or support lead to ineffective implementations, unmet expectations, and a change-resistant team that's passively working against you. By the time you get everyone up-to-speed, that new tech you've just invested in is reaching its end of life.

Are you in FOMO Adopter mode? We've all felt tired and frustrated by the accelerating pace of change. Before you jump into another hasty rollout, go for a beer with a Pragmatic Adopter and ask them what they're thinking. The best way to get out of the trap you're in is to jump ahead of the game and buy your team some much needed stability.

The Denier

Deniers denounce new technology until there's no other option, and even then they resist change as long as they can. They refuse to act until compliance demands it, customers insist on it, or the team flat-out refuses to keep using the clunky legacy workaround. Every industry has them. Every person has worked for one.

Deniers are often proud of their restraint. They view themselves as frugal, skeptical, and experienced. They're often late career and they've already weathered more change than most of us can possibly imagine. They've worked hard and earned their medals. They've earned the stability they're craving, even if it's not realistic.

Their advantage is that they wring every droplet of utility out of every piece of tech in their ecosystem. Their risk is that frugality often comes at a massive hidden cost to their business. In times of rapid disruption, the Denier risks falling out of step with how value is delivered, perceived, and experienced. By the time Deniers finally do act, catching up is twice as hard and three times as expensive. Even then, it may be too late.

Are you in Denier mode? It's time to be honest with yourself. What is your decision to do nothing really costing in terms of your finances, reputation, and business valuation? Is your choice really about what's best for the business, or is it hiding a personal need for stability?

Each of the four styles is completely understandable. They all come from the same place: a deep desire to protect the business you have built. That's a good instinct. Remind yourself frequently that protecting the business doesn't mean change is inherently bad or good. It means change will happen, and you are responsible for shaping it.

It's also worth noting that you may employ different styles at the same time. It's actually quite common for a leader to embrace the latest technology related to their craft, while remaining sceptical of the need to innovate in other areas of the business.

No matter which technology mode you're in right now, the goal is simply to adopt from a smarter place. Accept that your style simply describes the intersection of your current situation and your lived experiences. You need a framework for evaluating and implementing technological changes in your business that confirms whether your instinctive reaction is the right one.

That's exactly what we're about to build. But first, let me tell you what happened when I was first introduced to AI.

How Caution Almost Derailed My Business

I've spent the majority of my career in either Blind Adopter or Pragmatic Adopter mode. But when AI emerged on scene, I was deeply sceptical. Something about the AI hype-cycle triggered my internal Denier. "How arrogant and self-important you must be" I thought, "to believe that you are so smart as to improve on the human brain, when medical science has barely scratched the surface of its function."

My attitude was quite simple. Prove it, or be quiet.

Then I was introduced to Megan. A very confident young woman with a deep passion for this emerging technology. She made me a bet. She would prove to me that AI could do my job. Equally confident that it couldn't but willing to find out for sure, I took the bet. What followed was eye opening for both of us. We were both right. And we were both wrong.

AI cannot do my job. My lived experience is inaccessible to any internet data store. My sharp intuition is more complex than an algorithm. But there are aspects of my work that AI does much better than I do, at much faster speeds. These tend to also be the things that bog me down, burning up time that would be more productively spent doing something else. AI also makes it possible for me to be present for clients in ways that were previously impossible.

Had I not taken that bet, I would still be sitting at my desk with my arms crossed, silently terrified. Because I set aside my scepticism and embraced a risk-free pilot project, I unlocked an entirely new chapter in my business and professional life. I moved from Denier to Pragmatic Adopter overnight, and dramatically enhanced the value I deliver for my clients. That's the difference between thoughtful caution and passive resistance. One keeps you aware, engaged, and in control. The other leaves you vulnerable, stagnating, and bordering on irrelevance.

Caution Isn't Your Enemy

Let's put this myth to bed before we move on. In our modern-day business discourse, popular culture tends to mock the cautious entrepreneur in favor of his cool, younger brother, hustle. A 2024 paper published by DIW Berlin[14] showed that entrepreneurs with moderate risk tolerance outperformed both high and low risk types in terms of profitability and survival.

An appropriate level of caution is a sign of wisdom hard-earned. It's a reflection of your lived experience and is shaped by how close you've come to the edge. By how many people (and their families) count on you getting it right. Every decision carries weight.

That weight makes risk real. Personal. Sometimes even paralysing. So no, risk aversion is not a problem. It's a healthy response to an unknown. Problems only arise when fear of risk convinces you that *not deciding* is safer than deciding imperfectly. That is never true.

Your Technology Engine Starts With Your Business

Throughout history, technology has been used for things human beings either can't or don't want to do. It is most advantageous when it replaces structured, manual tasks that can be broken down into a series of repeatable steps. It easily replaces routine work or work that is either slow or physically difficult for humans. Because it never gets bored, it's also more accurate at these routine tasks. Modern AI takes this advantage to an entirely new level.

However, if the system you are replacing is already broken, technology will only amplify your problems. Despite our many attempts to prove otherwise, it has consistently failed to replace human intelligence, intuition, and critical thinking. Even in the age of AI. This is because all technologies are bound by the same basic constraints — they are limited by the critical thinking and biases of the human beings who created them.

Great technology decisions start with business problems, not platforms, specs or pricing sheets. The strongest tech stacks deliver measurable improvement in either capacity or customer experience. That is the mission of your Technology Engine.

Components of your Technology Engine

At a high level, your technology engine is made up of the same three buckets – your team, your tools, and your touchpoints. However, the structure they take is different. This is because your technology stack doesn't exist in a silo. Most systems span more than one area of your business and are impacted by the needs of multiple decision makers.

Your Technology Team

If you have an in-house CIO and IT team, they will manage the external relationships and logistical considerations of your IT stack, working in partnership with the end users inside the organization. However, most small businesses lack the budget for this level of support.. The oversight role typically falls to either operations or finance, and it's function is coordinating all the systems you are using, weighing in on total cost of ownership, compatibility and possible redundancies. Each department usually has one person who is designated to "manage" functional systems at a department level. Your CRM or your accounting platform are common examples – who owns data integrity and customizations to the platform?

You should also have some form of external IT support provider who takes care of network security, keeps your computer systems running and virus free, and supports you on major hardware or software purchases. Go back through your org chart and identify the people in your organization who fill these roles within the context of their jobs, and note which role is a technology driver for each team.

Your Technology Touchpoints

This is where things get interesting. Every time an employee, a customer, or a vendor engages your business through a digital platform, they represent a technology engine touchpoint. Those touchpoints will either make it easier for the user to achieve their goal and accelerate your business, or they will add friction and barriers that slow down your progress. This is your reminder to stay aware of their needs and their experiences. A clunky toolset that diminishes morale is as damaging as a bad website experience to your customer relationships.

Your Technology Tools

These are the software and hardware behind the systems that operate your business. The options are too varied to address comprehensively here. As a rule, include your internal network, any centralized storage (whether in the cloud or in-house), internet connections, phone systems, software, and any external platforms you either host or access, such as your websites and customer portals. As a smaller firm, you may have a centralized technology budget that everyone draws from. Larger organizations will often allocate departmental technology budgets, even though management oversight is best centralized.

A Leader's Guide to Technology Decisions

As the owner of the business, you have both a financial interest and a fiduciary interest in the technology decisions made by your organization. Which is a fancy way of saying that what matters to you comes down to two simple things: does the benefit of the technology outweigh the cost of deploying it, and are there sufficient safeguards in place to protect you from legal or reputational risk as a result of the platform's use?

Once you have satisfied yourself that the answer to these questions is yes, unless you take great pleasure from tinkering with programs and setting up networks, your wisest course of action is to leave implementation and management to the subject matter experts you have hired to do this work. The hours you will waste fiddling with network settings and IT troubleshooting are much more profitably used generating income in your business.

That will be our focus for the rest of this chapter – empowering you with a structured process to identify technology gaps and opportunities, prioritize them, establish the requirements of a solution, and then evaluate the options before making a buying decision.

Identify Technology Gaps & Opportunities

We'll assume your business already has a working technology stack, everyone on your team has access to the hardware necessary to do their work and you have a centralized inventory of all the hardware, software, and subscriptions you use. If you don't have these basics in place, start with an inventory of what you do have.

We're going to focus on the gaps and opportunities you can leverage to accelerate your growth. It's time get uncomfortably specific about the friction points in your business. We call these chokepoints. They are the places where relationships become strained, work gets stalled, or time is wasted. Make a list of every chokepoint you are aware of, then ask your leadership team to do the same. For each chokepoint, work backwards from the friction point until you land on the root cause. You will sort these causes into three buckets – automate, augment, and other.

When that root cause is due to repetitive tasks that waste time and cause backlogs, routine work that could easily be automated, or backlogs due to team capacity, technology is a good option to solve it. However, when the core process itself is breaking down, technology won't solve it. Fix the process first, then automate.

Other friction points don't trace directly back to technology, but still present an opportunity to improve the customer experience through augmentation. For example, client onboarding that is handled entirely through one-on-one meetings might be more effective if certain components were offered through on-demand training that clients could take on their own time, supplemented by a smaller number of virtual meetings where they could ask questions and get targeted support. Self-service support options might provide instant solutions to common problems while also reducing wait times at your call center.

Other times, what initially feels like a technology problem is actually a people problem in disguise. When that's the case, it doesn't matter how much you invest in a technology solution, it won't fix the real problem. However, it will add complexity and introduce new failure points.

You should now have two lists: problems that can and should be solved by technology and people/process problems that should be approached as such. You know what to do with the people and process problems. The answers are all in your operational alignment plan. We're going to focus on the technology problems here.

Prioritize Initiatives

By now, you've probably amassed a list of goals for your technology implementation, but what should you tackle first. Start by estimating the impact on your business of eliminating each chokepoint. Will it boost morale? Increase customer satisfaction? Reduce costs? Improve sales success?

Next, assign a dollar value to solving each problem. For example, if customers are happier and that reduces your churn rate by 5%, how would that impact your revenue over the next 12 months? What is the capacity impact of solving each problem? How much time and attention will your employees gain back when you solve this issue.

Finally, organize your projects so that the ones that have the strongest overall benefit to the organization are the top of the list. Get really clear on which of your projected outcomes will move the needle for your business and focus there. Everything else is noise in the form of a sales pitch.

If you are still unsure where to begin, start by streamlining work that is repetitive, rules-based, or administrative. Automating these tasks will reduce error rates and increase your team's capacity to do other, higher value work, both of which are a net benefit to your company.

A little human psychology can be invaluable here. If a chokepoint that is particularly irritating to either your customers or your staff can be solved quickly and relatively inexpensively, it should almost always be first. The goodwill effect of fixing that problem creates positive momentum that will smooth the path for the more complex work ahead.

Establish Solution Requirements

You've now answered the "what" of technology realignment. It's time to begin deciding how. As the business leader, your focus should be on the outcomes you need from a solution to the problem. What are the outcomes the solution must deliver? What are the nice-to-haves that would add measurable impact and improve ROI? Which results would be ideal in a perfect world, but can be addressed in other ways without a significant loss of value from the core solution.

The answers to these questions are sometimes called business user requirements – they are the non-technical descriptions of what you need the solution to accomplish. You will evaluate possible purchases based on how well they meet each of these criteria.

Evaluate and Choose a Solution

With your requirements list in hand, it's time to recruit help. This could be a project champion you assign from your internal team or an external consultant or IT specialist you hire to guide you through the selection process. Their job is to present you with a shortlist of options that check all your dealbreaker needs and meet at least 80% of your priority nice-to-have requirements on paper. Any less and you are likely to end up with another layer of workarounds in very short order. They should also take stock of your existing tech stack to be sure you can't solve the problem using something you've already bought and support you through negotiations with your chosen vendor(s) to get the best deal possible for your organization.

Once you have made a decision and signed a contract with your chosen vendor, implementation is best left to the experts. As the leader, your job is to establish the success criteria and keep an eye on progress to be sure those criteria are met.

Extend the Life of Your Tech Stack

Technology has become one of the major costs of doing business, so it makes sense to get as much value as you can from every purchase. Consider where you expect your business to be in three to five years' time and make your selection with this longer term lens in mind. The last thing you want is to drag your team through the frustration of a steep learning curve only to start the process all over again the minute they begin to feel they've mastered a new system.

Most businesses also have existing legacy systems that aren't going anywhere, such as your accounting platform or perhaps an ERP. Any solutions that are unable to work alongside or integrate with these systems could cause more problems than they solve, and are rarely worth the pain that results.

Don't Skimp on Training and Onboarding

The business world is littered with incomplete software implementations that died on the vine because the team was either unwilling or unable to use them. Technology adoption isn't real unless your people are willing to change their way of doing work in order to gain the advantages that the technology offers. When they understand the *why*, not just the *how*, they are more likely to accept changes to "the way we've always done things."

This means training with context, and monitoring adoption. During training, don't just focus on which buttons to click. Demonstrate how this tool improves *their* day, *their* workflow, *their* outcomes. If you focus only on functionality, you increase the risk that your fancy new tech stack gets used minimally, or not at all. Once training is complete, check in regularly to ensure no unexpected workarounds are creeping into your workflows.

On one call with my client James, his new sales rep was proudly showing off a stack of spreadsheets he had created in order to track contract dates. Tired of digging through endless files for each client, he had created a series of spreadsheets to keep track of contract data, using them to manually send reminder emails and trigger renewal outreach. It had never occurred to him that he could store that data in the CRM, allowing renewal tasks and emails to be automated. A simple tweak that took 15 minutes to implement freed up dozens of administrative hours each month that could be dedicated to prospecting. A much better use of a sales rep's time, don't you think?

We've Done Fine Without It This Far

Sometimes, instead of solving a known problem, technology creates an entirely new category. Before 1994, no business anywhere had ever said "We need a website." No teenager before 2007 begged for an iPhone for Christmas. The same is true for GenAI and AI agents. When these leaps forward happen, you need another way to stay grounded without shutting down progress.

The next time a completely new technology enters the conversation, invite your leadership team to pause and ask three deceptively simple questions:

- **How could this fit into what we already do?** When technology helps you do something faster, better, or cheaper without breaking what already works, it's worth exploring.

- **What's now possible that wasn't before?** When technology unlocks a new capability, business model, or service stream that creates real customer value, it can be a game changer for your future.

- **What opportunity does this reveal that we haven't thought of?** The most strategic leaders I work with are the ones willing to explore the white space, to experiment with small bets that test new assumptions and reveal hidden value.

Just remember to stay grounded in the capacity your business has to weather the change. The right innovation at the right time could lead you to disrupt your entire industry. But a powerful tool at the wrong time will do little more than disrupt your business.

Key Takeaway

Technology is a multiplier. It amplifies whatever system it's applied to, regardless of whether that system is good or bad. Plug it into a disorganized process and you'll just get chaos at scale. Used well, technology will absolutely fuel your competitive advantage. But to succeed, it has to support your strategy and be rolled out in alignment with your digital maturity, culture, and capacity.

HOW ALEX REALIGNED HIS BUSINESS

Once they realized that the online learning assets they had created were a scalable opportunity, Alex's team got to work on their Growth Clarity Blueprint. Using it, they expanded the training programs so that the ideas were easier to implement and turned them into paid courses companies could license. They also recreated their free courses so that they served as an entry point into the paid programs. Better yet, they used those same free courses to introduce the firm to an entirely new market.

Before going all-in, Alex and his team pressure-tested their ideas with a controlled test. Response was positive. The trainings were affordable and easy to digest, making them a no-brainer for CMOs looking to do more work in-house but afraid of losing the expertise of their agency partners. And a few clients who bought the training pilot hired Alex's company for projects they realized they couldn't do well in-house.

Based on these early positive results, Alex invested in the learning platforms and tools he would need to deliver training at scale. He standardized processes and restructured his team to ensure individual priorities were clear. Finally, Alex doubled down on webinars, guest speaking, and industry roundtables to make sure his ideal clients knew their training programs existed. Within months, the learning platform was generating consistent revenue and additional projects continued to trickle in.

8 COMMON MISTAKES THAT HINDER GROWTH

As we come to the end of Act II: Realign, there are a few common traps that I see business leaders fall into when they go it alone and implement their Growth Architecture Framework without support. I don't want you to be one of them. I've assembled this list of the most common ways to derail your growth, so that you can be proactive about avoiding them.

Mistake #1: Confusing Reallocation with Retrenchment

Have you ever asked yourself "What can I live without to keep the things I desperately need?" That's a retrenchment mindset. To win amid chaos, it's crucial to shift your mindset from retrenchment to strategic reallocation. Instead of trying to do more with less, focus on doing what matters most with what you have. This subtle mental shift starts by asking, "Given everything we know now, what's the most important use of our time, money, and people?" This simple question moves your focus from cost-cutting to resource optimization.

Mistake #2: Ignoring the Leaks

It's hard to maintain growth while your resources are seeping away without generating returns. For most businesses, these leaks aren't hidden. They're right there in all the minor nuisances and annoying hurdles you've chosen to just live with because fixing them feels like too much work. Time wasted on redundant processes. Machinery that keeps breaking down. Sluggish software that traps people staring at a screen watching a little wheel turn endlessly. These seemingly minor annoyances aren't just inefficiencies. They're expensive distractions that waste time. Sometimes you need to rip off the bandage and suffer the pain of fixing them.

Mistake 3: Not Knowing When to Cut, Protect, or Amplify

Not every possible leak is a straightforward decision. That client who's not profitable might happily pay a higher fee once they understand where you are coming from. Take the time you need to have clarity on your decision before you start to make cuts. For my business advisory clients, that clarity often comes from sorting their efforts into three buckets.

- **Cut:** Let go of anything (or anyone) that's draining you without delivering value in return. This isn't about punishing teams or slashing budgets indiscriminately. It's about recognizing when something has outlived its usefulness and having the courage to stop it.
- **Protect:** Hold steady on those things that will carry you forward. Your best people. Your loyal customer relationships. Your brand trust. Your revenue engine. These are assets that take years to build yet only moments to lose and forever to recover.

- **Amplify:** If something is working, give it more. More room. More budget. More time. More support. Especially if it's aligned with where the market is going, not just where it's been.

Mistake #4: Leading with Your Budget

Your comptroller or accountant will lead with the numbers. They should. But remember their job is to look in the rearview mirror. You need to remain focused on where you're going, and leading with your budget is a surefire way to operate from a place of scarcity. Because when your eyes are turned to the past, every dollar invested is a dollar removed from your nest egg. It's an approach that's sure to get you into trouble.

As you are working through implementing your framework, ask "does this thing that we do contribute to or support the things we want to protect or amplify?" Only consider cutting if the answer is no. Otherwise, focus on how to make it happen with the resources you have. It's one thing to see possible trouble ahead and think through the decisions you'll make if, and when, you have to. It's entirely another to make those decisions reactively out of fear, long before they're necessary.

Mistake #5: Not Viewing Talent as a Strategic Resource

When things get tight, it's easy to look at headcount through the lens of cost. The thing is, your team isn't just a line item, it's the engine that drives your growth. A common way this shows up is deciding to eliminate a leadership role and pick that mantle back up yourself. Usually a sales manager or a marketing director. Under pressure, you overlook the reason you hired that person in the first place. Or worse, tell yourself it was a mistake. Except leading that function isn't your core strength. Pretty soon, results flatline, momentum stalls and you're mired back in the trap of putting out fires.

Any time a team member leaves, they inevitably take with them some proprietary knowledge of how your company operates. Not the numbered lists of steps in your process manual, the kind of knowledge that only comes from being part of the team. Some of that insight is critical operational memory you don't personally share, and it will be impossible to recover.

Discipline yourself to view your people as key partners, not merely executors of tasks. They represent investments you have made and relationships you have nurtured. Be careful not to toss away their long-term value for short-term gain.

Mistake #6: Inflexible Plans & Rigid Operating Models

If the last few years have shown us anything, it's that volatility is now the baseline. Static budgets and rigid operating models will leave you overcommitted in all the wrong places. You'll find yourself overburdened with rigid systems, fixed goals that don't fit reality, and struggling to pivot in real time as the market changes. Your Blueprint is a 12-month roadmap with high level goals and milestones identified. Use it to create an action plan for just the next 90-days, building in a cadence of quarterly sprints followed by reflection and redirection. As you review your results and formalize your next 90-day priorities, you also have an opportunity to revisit your budget and ensure your investment remains in step with your anticipated returns.

Mistake #7: Hoarding Cash Without Investing Forward

Once you start building up your cash reserves, the temptation is often to bank them for a rainy day. Or maybe to invest in that dream car you've always wanted. Either way, it's tempting to divert as much of your profit as possible to build your personal wealth in the here and now. To be clear, you should be diverting some of that profit for this purpose. Decide ahead of time what percentage of your profit you will allocate to cash reserves, and what percentage you will set aside for investing in growth. Award your management bonuses and personal dividends only from what remains after those two buckets have been filled. This ensures that you retain the resilience your business needs to whether future storms.

Mistake #8: Outsourcing Decision-Making

Of all the mistakes that you can make with your business, this one is the deadliest. It's also the most common under stress. Here's what it looks like:

You have an idea you think will help your business – it could be a project or an advisor you want to work with. But it's an investment you hadn't planned on, so before you commit, you try to derisk the decision by getting a second opinion. And here's where you introduce the biggest risk of all.

Given the opportunity, it's human nature to consider what's best for ourselves in any situation. The feedback you get from others will be affected by how your decision might impact them personally. What's best for them won't necessarily align with what's best for you or your business. Only you can make that choice.

You might still want a second opinion, so make sure it has value by asking a better question. Any opinions you solicit from employees or contractors should be specific to their role, and used only to help you validate a decision you've already made. For example:

- Ask your accountant *how* you can pay for this, not whether you should invest the money. If you absolutely can't afford it, they'll tell you anyway.

- Ask your COO *how* you can organize your business to accommodate it. They'll tell you what's needed and where the risks are. Then you decide if it's worth it.

- Ask your business coach to help you *work through a decision*, not for permission to move. They are your advisor, not your parent.

I was amazed at how much resistance vanished from my agency's progress when I stopped waiting for consensus. It turned out that everything I wanted to do was eminently achievable, once it became clear to my team that I was comfortable as the captain of my ship.

Do Any of These Feel Familiar?

Chances are good you've come across at least one of them, either in your own business or in someone else's. Leave that in the past. Now that you're aware of the traps that await you, you can make a conscious choice to avoid them. We're going to introduce tools to help you in the next section, Act III: Reinvent.

ACT III: REINVENT

You will make better decisions when you proactively stay ahead of the curve.

12

LEADERSHIP DEFINES YOUR FUTURE

Your work on realignment should take no more than 90 days of your focused attention. That doesn't mean the work is done. It most likely isn't. It does mean that your senior team should be able implement the rest of your plan with minimal supervision, freeing you up to focus on what's next. The good news? Now that you've done the hard work to stabilize your business, you've dramatically increased your chances of surviving this moment of crisis. The bad news is that if you stop now, you are still vulnerable to the same challenges when the next one hits.

Your next decision is the most important one you will make. What will you do now that the wolf is no longer at the door? Will you double down on what's familiar, hoping the next storm will pass you by? Or will you take this opportunity to reinvent how your organization connects to customer value, so that over time you build a business that is both crisis-proof and future-ready?

This moment right now is an inflection point. The only way to truly thrive over the long-term is to commit your organization to the hard work of staying relevant. That work starts at the top.

The Impact of Leadership

Your fortunes depend on the strength and structure of your Leadership Engine — the interconnected roles, reporting structures, and management systems that shape every decision, priority, and cultural signal in your organization. When leadership engines fail, businesses quietly stall out.

I've encountered three common leadership traps that show up at this point in my work with founders. Unchecked, they will cause your momentum to stall and your growth to backslide. Fortunately, there are ways to avoid all three.

Some founders try to do it all themselves. They either worry they can't afford strong leaders on their payroll or they're convinced that they alone understand their business well enough to make good operational decisions.

Others don't fully buy into customer obsession. Willing to tolerate change in a crisis, the moment our work is done, they slowly, silently drag their team back to the old, familiar way of operating. The first tiny bump in the road becomes the excuse they've been waiting for. All progress is abandoned as they drag their demoralized teams into the past.

The third most common trap is believing that people can figure the rest out for themselves. Left to their own devices, these leadership teams learn through trial and (expensive) error. They work longer and harder, pull out all the stops and expect their staff to do likewise. The result is a culture of overwork that views stress and long hours as a badge of commitment.

In all three cases, the outcome is the same. Founders and owners find themselves perpetually dragged back into the minutiae of day-to-day operations. Top players begin to leave and those that stay start to burn out, creating a demoralized team and a potentially toxic culture. As all the gains begin to slip away, these founders — trapped and busy putting out fires — miss the early warning signs and quickly find themselves embroiled in the next crisis. With a bottleneck at the top and anarchy at the bottom, the business stagnates, rotting slowly from the inside out.

No founder consciously sets out to undermine their business. They are driven by the same psychological forces we talked about in Act I: Rethink. The urge to fall into one of these three traps is alive and well inside each and every one of us. In order to build a business that is truly crisis-proof and future-ready, we must each make an effort to overcome them.

That work began when you made a conscious choice to embed customer obsession into every fibre of your business. Not as a project, but as an ambient condition that influences every decision, every process, and every role inside your organization.

It will take leadership and discipline to permanently shift the way your business operates, securing long-term stability and the freedom you've been looking for from the very beginning of your entrepreneurial journey. In the chapters that follow, we'll walk through how to make reinvention real.

You will restore confidence. Because before you can move forward, your people must trust both the direction and the leader setting it. We'll explore how to rebuild morale, restore your team's sense of purpose, and lead from a place of clarity and conviction. You've been through a war together. Emotional recovery is the prerequisite for continuing growth.

You'll install a crisis-proof business model. Structure matters. If the business relies on your presence to function, it's not resilient, it's fragile. We'll introduce a cadence of planning, review, and accountability that empowers your team to make decisions quickly and align around what matters most. This is how strategy gets operationalized.

Next, you'll move from crisis-proof to future-ready. We'll look at how to build a culture of anticipation, not just reaction. We'll explore how to spot early signals of change, when to pivot, and how to align future-facing innovation with your core customer promise. Being future-ready is more than a defensive play. It's how you continue to lead through uncertain times.

Reinvention isn't a project, it's a muscle. Act III is where you build it. The strength of your leadership is what will drive it. So as you work through the next few chapters, remember this: you don't have to fix everything alone, but you *do* have to lead the shift. Are you ready?

13

REBUILD CONFIDENCE TO ENGAGE YOUR MARKET

You've already survived what many don't. That's not hyperbole. It's reality. Surviving a business crisis takes strength, tenacity, creativity, and an extraordinary tolerance for ambiguity. As soon as the dust settles, a new challenge begins. This one is less visible, but just as critical.

Recovery.

You're already on your way to financial recovery and operational continuity. I'm talking about psychological and strategic recovery.

As a leader, you need to restore your confidence in yourself, your business, and your market. Without it, you will leave your business vulnerable to fear-based decision-making, even when on the surface it looks like things are going well. I've seen the effects play out time and again in the businesses I advise. On the surface, recovery is going well. Under the hood?

- Profits are poured into eliminating debt and restoring cash reserves as quickly as possible, with nothing set aside to invest in the continued growth of the business.
- Key hires are postponed at the expense of capacity.

- Strategic efforts are watered down in favor of conserving cash for another downturn.

Even though the business is stabilized and in strong financial health, every bump in the road triggers a resurgence of the stress associated with the crisis. That brings back all the same instinctive behaviors that got you in trouble to begin with.

And, yes, I've made all of these mistakes myself. Often with the full backing of my financial advisors. You'll know this is happening to you when you find yourself in a pattern of crisis and recovery that seems to repeat over and over again.

The Chaos Hangover Is Real

What happens to leaders after a crisis isn't something most people talk about. At least not openly. Although the numbers have started to stabilize, something inside you may not. You've been to the precipice of disaster and looked over the cliff. An inner voice whispers *"What if it happens again? What if I can't stop it next time?"*

That voice doesn't make you weak. It makes you human.

Surviving chaos is a form of trauma. You've fought to keep your business alive. You've lost good people. You've stared down bills you weren't sure you could pay. You've said good-bye to clients you couldn't afford to lose. That leaves a mark.

Once you're technically "safe," everyone assumes you'll just bounce back to the growth-oriented, optimistic, energized leader who entered the chaos. You're expected to keep charging forward as though nothing scary ever happened. But that's not how trauma works.

In reality, your body stays in fight-or-flight mode. You become hypervigilant for any sign that the monster might return, scanning the horizon for danger even when the sky looks clear. You have a healthy bank balance, but you're terrified to invest in growth. You double down on short-term wins instead of long-term positioning, because you can't shake the feeling that your safety is temporary.

The worst part? You can't talk about it. Not to your team. Not to your peers. Sometimes, you can't even admit it to yourself. You worry that if you admit you're still shaken, others might think you're not up to the task.

Enter toxic optimism in the form of coaches and advisors telling you to suck it up. They dismiss your fears and tell you to "stop being negative," to "choose abundance," to "get back to work." All things you'd really love to do, if only you could remember what that felt like.

Here's the thing. Those coaches? They're wrong. Ignoring a chaos hangover doesn't build confidence. It buries fear under a cloak of bravado. Real confidence comes from somewhere else.

Successful entrepreneurs don't simply get over it. They choose to move forward by deliberately and methodically building toward something stronger, wiser, and more resilient than what came before. Let's dive into how you can cultivate that kind of confidence in yourself, in your team, and in the market.

First, Accept the Message Beneath the Crisis

More often than not, a business crisis is the result of external forces beyond your control: geopolitical shifts, market disruptions, changes in consumer expectations, or emerging competitors with lower-cost models. These forces can make your existing value proposition appear less relevant or overpriced, even when the underlying value remains strong.

The market's **perception** of your value has simply changed in light of new options, new norms, or new limitations. And it could happen again.

Accepting that external forces can reframe how your value is perceived is the first step to rebuilding confidence. This kind of disruption is inevitable and likely to happen many more times throughout the life of your business. Once you've accepted this as true, your struggles instantly become less personal. That clears the path for you to take action and rebuild confidence in your leadership.

Next, Rewire Your Subconscious

As long as your mind and body are hard-wired in survival mode, you'll second-guess every decision, play small when you should step up, and subtly communicate fear to your team and your market. To build a strong leadership engine, you must first reset your own internal posture.

This isn't about faking positivity. People who know you well will see right through that fake, pasted on smile. You'll gain more confidence by deliberately grounding yourself in strength, truth, and capability. Here are some strategies that have worked both for me and for my clients.

- **Hire a thoughtful executive advisor who sees the whole picture.** This isn't the time for a cheerleader or a tactical integrator evangelizing a rigid structure of systems and processes. You need someone with firsthand experience of the emotional and strategic complexity of where you've been, and the freedom awaiting you when you get where you want to go. Someone who makes it safe to confront the reality of what's working, what needs healing, and what new ground you can stand on.

- **Surround yourself with a community that 'Gets It'.** Find a group of peers who understand the stakes. This could be an industry association, a mastermind group, or a few good friends who also own businesses that you meet for drinks every other Friday night. It might be a paid circle or a casual network. As long as you have a trusted circle of people who've been through it or are still in it, who won't flinch when you say, *"I'm exhausted,"* or *"I'm scared to hire again."* These relationships help keep you grounded and moving forward. They remind you that you're not broken, you're rebuilding.

- **Take consistent daily action.** Remember action bias? Make it work for you. Confidence grows when it's rooted in evidence. That evidence comes from action. Commit to taking small, consistent steps every day. Pause at the end of each day to acknowledge your progress, no matter how small it seems.

When you repeatedly make small choices well and stay the course, your body starts to believe it. Over time, these tiny actions will retrain your nervous system to feel confidence in place of survival instinct.

- **Pay attention to your attention.** We live in a world where algorithms designed to monetize our fear and outrage are everywhere. Today's news cycle isn't built to inform you, it's designed to lure you in and keep you watching. The problem is that when you're vulnerable, it's easy to mistake all that noise for reality. One of the smartest things you can do is to reclaim your perspective by reducing your exposure and taking back control of where your attention goes. Trade that morning social media scroll for time spent taking the actions that support your progress.

- **Keep a wins diary.** At the end of the day, instead of doom-scrolling, take a few minutes to note every positive signal you experienced. Every goal reached. Every win, no matter how tiny. When you find your attention slipping into pessimism or fear, pull out your notebook and read through as many pages as necessary to shift your attention from fear to possibility.

These aren't dramatic interventions. They're quiet, consistent acts of personal leadership. They're what give you the capacity to rebuild, not just your business, but your own belief in it.

You didn't go through this fire alone however. So, while you're quietly rebuilding your own center, it's wise to invest some time to rebuild the confidence within your team.

Rebuild Team Confidence

As soon as your own foundation starts to feel steadier, turn outward towards your team. They felt the tremors too. They saw what you saw. Some of them absorbed more of it than you realized. Just like you, they need evidence that the worst is behind them.

The first step to rebuilding trust and belief is to be sure your leadership team is on board. That starts by openly admitting that the last while has been chaotic. Name the grind you've been through together. Call out the effort they have made and thank them for their support. Then reset the tone with honest optimism that focuses attention on the future and the opportunities ahead of you. Find a way to celebrate how far you've already come. Then do the same thing again with the entire organization.

Here, clarity wins over rah-rah leadership. Your people don't crave motivational slogans and impassioned speeches. They do need to know where your business stands, what matters now, and what success looks like in the short term. Be as transparent as you are comfortable being. Let people know the basic metrics you are tracking and where those numbers need to be to support *their personal goals.* This both motivates them and helps them feel reassured that everything is moving in the right direction.

It's important to stay present as a leader, now more than ever. The more uncertainty your staff feels, the more your steadiness matters. Talk to them. Share openly about the future you envision. Congratulate them on their wins or invite them to share challenges they're facing and how they're approaching the solutions. The confidence you demonstrate through your words and actions will be contagious.

Use that confidence to stimulate momentum. Prioritize early, visible wins that will help your team believe sustained progress is possible. Build in routines that share these wins publicly. Some companies do this through a daily standup. Others have a company-wide slack channel where congratulations are shared. Others send a regular staff newsletter. The logistics matter less than consistency. Find a routine that works with your organization's culture and size. Then stick with it.

These actions aren't dramatic. They literally take days, not months, to make happen and they do wonders to set the stage for what comes next.

Rebuilding Market Confidence

In Act II: Realign, you did the hard work of repositioning your business and rebuilding your revenue engine around what your customers value most. Now it's time to live that positioning with consistency and credibility.

Chances are good that in the middle of the chaos, you either pulled back on marketing or your messaging got a bit confusing. That's left your customers wondering, even if they won't say so out loud. The thing is confused clients hesitate, they don't buy.

Your customers, partners, and your community need you to reinforce your relevance and reassure them of your integrity. Simply showing up with vulnerability paired with clarity will rebuild trust faster than any PR campaign. These five reputation-building moves will help you do just that.

Begin by intentionally reintroducing yourself. Your company has changed. Own the shift. Update your about page and relaunch your newsletter. As you do, clearly state who you are now, what you stand for, and what your customers can expect. You might even send a personal note to key stakeholders who work for your clients and partners. This isn't about fanfare. It's about transparency.

Lead with empathy, not urgency. Your longtime customers want to know that you still understand them, that you are here to help them in new and better ways than ever before. Reach out with questions, not pitches. Use softer, service-focused language, proactive check-ins, and low-stakes conversations to re-establish yourself as a partner and introduce new ways of working together.

Share what you're seeing and learning. Stories are the most human communication channel we have. Use your stories to offer insight and reflect on what's changing. Tell them what you see coming and how you are preparing for it. Share observations from the work you did to define your landscape and your community. When you become a voice of clarity, your relevance instantly rises.

I'm doing this myself as I write this book. Having recognized my strengths in navigating through times of turbulence, I'm redefining how I show up as a business performance advisor in contrast to the trite, canned growth strategy that clutters the internet. The work is similar, but the context has changed. If I don't acknowledge that, I too risk becoming irrelevant.

Reconnect with your champions. This is the perfect opportunity to reengage with past clients, collaborators, and referral partners who sing your praises. They are your most accessible bridge to rebuilding market visibility. Engage them with honesty and curiosity. Share your evolution and give them the tools they need to introduce you to people who need your help. It's up to you to teach them to recognize the places you can help their networks, places they may never have thought about.

Share generously what the crisis taught you. Teaching is positioning. It says: *We've been through it. We've thought deeply about it. We can help you navigate it, too.* Share what you've learned through blog posts, webinars, workshops, or even just a candid video. Hold roundtables or interviews that give you the opportunity to listen without pitching, helping you stay aligned with the market's evolving needs.

These five moves will help you step back into the market confidently, with your eyes open, your voice steady, and your message clear.

Key Takeaway

Looking successful on the outside doesn't mean you're feeling confident on the inside. The chaos hangover might be real, but it doesn't control your future. You do. You're stronger than you know. And maybe, just maybe, you're more ready than you have ever been.

HOW ALEX RESTORED CONFIDENCE

Even though the steps he had taken to introduce their new services had restored the market's confidence in his firm, Alex found himself struggling with his own equilibrium. He had come very close to losing his house during the crisis, and he just didn't feel safe. Fortunately, he'd begun meeting regularly with an advisor who supported him to take consistent, daily action and make moderate investments that didn't put his financial stability at risk.

Alex also noticed an undercurrent of fear lingering in the behavior of his team. He held a company-wide meeting to formally introduce the new division, making sure everyone understood how it fit into their future with the company. That meeting opened the door for candid conversations and quelled anxiety about job security. These small steps created the conditions Alex needed to be sure his company became both crisis-proof and future-ready.

14

BUILD A CRISIS-PROOF BUSINESS MODEL

You've accepted that change is inevitable and owned the chaos-hangover. Your next step is to ensure you have the flexibility to adapt to new shifts as they come. This chapter will provide you with a framework to integrate adaptability and resilience into your organizational culture, so that you can easily navigate the next period of chaos without hoping things will go back to how they were. Because they won't.

True resilience is meeting payroll, delivering on your promises, paying yourself a reasonable salary, and continuing to invest in your future, even when the world outside your walls is unstable. The most reliable path to that world is tailoring everything about your business to continually meet your ideal customers' emerging and unrealized needs. What you've done so far isn't the end of the journey. It's the beginning of a new way of operating.

This work starts with the design of your leadership engine – the tools, the team and the touchpoints that drive decision-making in your organization.

Start With Your Leadership Team

You can't have a crisis-proof business if your leadership engine is under-resourced. When you worked through realignment, you identified roles on your org chart to lead the core functions of your revenue engine, your operations engine, and your technology engine. In an ideal world, you want one individual to own the performance of each of those engines. It is their responsibility to manage the day-to-day activities of their team, keep you informed of progress towards your goals, and alert you quickly to any risks or challenges.

Take a moment to revisit those decisions. Have you identified the strongest candidate to own each of these functions? If leadership has been split between different individuals, are you clear who owns what outcomes? Are they? Your leadership team will be only as effective as the clarity you provide them permits, never more.

For most small and mid-sized businesses, the internal leadership team typically includes an operations leader (Director of Operations, GM, Operations Manager), a financial leader (often an external accountant or fractional CFO), a sales leader, and a marketing leader. In my experience, it's a rare unicorn who understands both the sales function and the marketing function – so these roles are generally better served by fractional leaders until your business is approaching or above $20 million ARR.

Until you are comfortably established in the 8-figure revenue club, bringing C-Suite roles in-house typically means one of two things. You've hired people without the experience you need, hoping the title will transform them. Or you are overinvesting in generals, unnecessarily hampering your ability to fund the army.

If your name still occupies multiple boxes on your org chart and your business is too small to justify a full leadership team, don't despair. You can build strategic advisory supports into your business without incurring the full cost of fractional leader. Most expert advisors offer entry-level engagements that provide you with limited access to their expertise. A good advisor will also help you delegate responsibility and authority to your team appropriately, so that you begin to build the organizational muscles that prepare you for a future where you are fully supported in leading your organization.

What About Leadership Tools and Touchpoints

The next crisis will come. That much is certain. Your job is to put the right model in place so that you are ready to capitalize on it. To do that, you will need to empower your leadership team with a very different collection of tools and touchpoints. These include:

- Making friends with your numbers through a solid grasp of your business performance data.
- Flexible processes and systems that bend without breaking, so that you can adapt quickly.
- Values-aligned leadership practices that yield stability and confidence, even during disruption.
- Rhythmic planning and internal engagement that guarantees you're never caught flat-footed again.

In order to build for tomorrow, you will calibrate your organizational structure, strategy, and leadership for a world where uncertainty is the norm, not the exception. Let's get started.

Make Friends With Your Numbers

Revenue is the lifeblood that flows through your business. If you don't understand how it's flowing, you're at risk of accidentally cutting through an artery. To have lasting peace of mind, you absolutely must know where your numbers stand at all times. This is why I start every new client engagement with a deep dive into their numbers. It gives me a clear picture of where things are flowing freely, and where there are blockages.

As founder, you have only two tasks, review the data and ask the hard questions. Your CFO or accountant can pull together much of the financial data you need, while your team leads should be able to provide the rest. Make them accountable and ask them to come prepared with suggested solutions to any key performance indicators (KPIs) that are not where they need to be.

When you know your numbers, you are better prepared to evaluate the many decisions that must be made. You will have more confidence to make strategic moves and the foresight to avoid investing beyond your capacity. For this reason, it's worth having a basic grasp of where they come from and what they tell you.

The math isn't complicated, but it does need to be grounded in reality. Use the calculators waiting for you in the resource center as a guide. Now let's take a look at the four types of numbers you will want to pay attention to.

Your Vital Signs

Your vital signs reassure you that your business remains solvent and help keep the chaos hangover at bay. When any of these numbers is off, it signals a crack appearing deeper in your model. Insist on receiving regular updates on the following metrics.

- What is your year-to-date (or quarter-to-date) income? (How does that compare to your goal?)
- What is your operating profit (or loss) over that same period? (Compared to your goal?)
- What is your cash on hand?
- What future revenue is expected from deals you have already closed?
- What is the gap between where you are and where you want to be by year end?

Review your vital signs in your regular metrics review sessions, following a cadence that matches the rhythm of your business. Consider a weekly review if you experience high volume sales with a short sales cycle. Choose either a bi-weekly or monthly schedule when your sales cycle is longer and your expenses are relatively predictable. More than a month between check-ins and you open the door for a leak to go unnoticed until it's too late.

Operating Efficiency Metrics

The numbers below show how efficiently you are operating, how much capacity you have to scale, and how effectively your revenue engine is working.

- What's your current sales volume, in units delivered?
- How many units can you sell if everyone is fully utilized at 80% billable?
- How many billable hours are you burning to deliver your current volume?
- What percentage of those hours are you actually billing?
- How long could you maintain operations if your revenue flatlined tomorrow?
- How many open opportunities are sitting in your sales pipeline? What percentage are likely to close?
- How long is your sales cycle?
- What's the average value of a new client contract?

Review your operating efficiency numbers quarterly with your broader team. We call these quarterly meetings "Plan-Do-Review Sessions" and you'll learn more about them later in this chapter.

Profitability Check-Up

Profitability check-ups help you surface issues with pricing, billing, and invoicing before they seriously disrupt your stability. The higher your sales volume, the more frequently you want to check these numbers. Most professional services firms will benefit from a monthly check-in, while product-driven organizations may be more comfortable with a quarterly review.

Your vital signs and operating efficiency metrics provide the inputs for your profitability check-up. Use them to answer the following questions.

- What are you *actually* being paid for each unit of output you are delivering? You will often find this number is not what your rate sheet says you're charging, especially in a professional or technical services firm.

- **What are your real margins?** Not the ones you planned on paper – the actual margins you're getting once real world inefficiencies are accounted for. Your actual margins should be fairly close to your planned margins and too much variance in either direction should be examined closely.

If you find you are delivering more than you are including in your price, recognize that you are squeezing your profit and blocking your ability to scale. Revisit the pricing section of Pillar 2: Operational Alignment for insight on what to do.

Where your operating margin is significantly higher than planned, it's important to do an integrity check. Are you cutting corners somewhere along the chain? Are promises being made but not kept? If these are true, then standards need to be enforced. On the other hand, if you're simply benefiting from efficiency as a result of your work to realign around customer obsession, congratulations. You've optimized your cost of goods and opened up capacity in your business to generate more income and profit with the resources you already have.

Future Cashflow Prediction

Your future cashflow signals how confidently you can invest in growth. Your CRM or ERP should be able to report your anticipated operating income over the next 90 days. It includes all guaranteed revenue from closed sales plus anticipated revenue from the opportunities in your sales pipeline, less the expenses associated with the goods you are selling and the fixed operating costs you anticipate over the same period.

Be sure to recognize how much of the income you project is from closed business (the contract is signed) versus anticipated business from active leads. Anticipated revenue is generally adjusted based on the probability that those deals are going to close, but it is an estimate and far from an exact science. If you have a 20% close ratio and one early stage deal worth $100,000 in the pipeline, you have a very different outlook than someone with the same close ratio who has five deals in the pipeline, each at various stages but only worth $20,000.

You may choose to make projections using only opportunities that are in the final stages of the sales process to increase your confidence in these numbers. This decision is entirely yours. The narrower your margins or the lower your risk tolerance, the more certainty you want.

When you are recovering from a crisis, a rolling 90-day cashflow prediction that you review at least monthly is invaluable for your peace of mind.

Embed Flexibility In Your Model

How can you reinvent your business to to flex, adapt, and thrive regardless of the external shocks you face? Flexibility is the core of a crisis-proof business, one that is modular, agile and portable. The goal is to move quickly and confidently when necessary because you've planned for the need to adapt. You'll accomplish this by embracing diversification combined with flexibility by design.

If you truly want to build a crisis-proof business, you must train yourself to focus on bending without breaking. I cannot stress this point enough. I have seen too many leaders struggle to survive a chaotic disruption only to starve their business of the resources it needs to fully recover, or panic and retreat each time they see a bump in the road ahead. Every time they do, they lose momentum, leak market share, and fall farther and farther behind their goals.

You already know change is inevitable. You've seen firsthand how external events can shift the ground beneath your business, sometimes overnight. The secret is to design for adaptability from the start. Your business model must be intentionally flexible, built to accommodate new realities without tearing everything down to the studs.

As we work through these components, keep in mind that there's a difference between strategic flexibility and reactive squirrel-chasing. Being adaptable won't come from chasing every trend or spinning in circles trying to reinvent yourself at every turn. Instead you're going to design your systems, structures, and operations in ways that allow you to make meaningful shifts without breaking your stride.

Diversification

In a crisis-proof business, diversification is foundational. When you rely too heavily on a single revenue stream, customer segment, market, or delivery model, you expose your business to unnecessary risk. If that one thing falters, your entire operation trembles.

Diversification gives you options to weather shifts in buying behavior, market sentiment, or economic pressure. The goal isn't to become everything to everyone. It's to build in the ability to pivot without starting from zero. You need to adapt quickly when conditions change.

During the pandemic, we saw companies that manufactured tenting pivot to producing face masks. Supply chains were restructured in response to shipping delays, reducing reliance on a single vendor or production facility. Retailers doubled down on ecommerce, offering click-and-collect models to reach consumers who no longer walked through their doors. In each case, success came from reimagining how their core capabilities could be applied to new needs or in different ways.

Diversification can take many forms, the most common of which are listed below:

- Can you offer new services to existing clients?
- Would tiered pricing or different packaging reach new market segments?
- How can you expand geographically?
- Where might you shift delivery channels (e.g., digital, self-serve, on-demand)?

The key is to diversify intentionally as a strategic way to increase resilience without diluting your focus. Done well, this will both protect your business and unlock new avenues for growth.

Start by looking for the opportunities that exist in business you already have. Does the value you deliver apply equally to a different customer segment without requiring you to restructure your current operating model? Are there elements of the work you do that could be offered as a stand-alone service? Are there new products and services adjacent to those you already offer that you could provide for your core market? Then, pick the most promising opportunity and begin the work of introducing it to your target market.

In my own business, as I began integrating AI knowledge and training more comprehensively into the way I was serving my advisory clients, I realized that the frameworks and strategic approaches I had developed offered significant value for a broader market of business leaders who may not be a fit for my core services. As I began talking openly about our human-centered, action-based AI programs, I engaged businesses outside my core market to attract a new revenue stream to my practice.

Flexibility by Design

A crisis-proof business is one that can change direction without collapsing under the weight of its own complexity. When you lead with the expectation that change is inevitable, you naturally design your business so it can evolve in place.

Remember the LEGO set you played with as a child? View your business the same way. Each function, process, or offering is a discrete, movable piece. If one breaks, it doesn't bring down the entire system. If a process becomes obsolete, it can be replaced or modernized. When a new opportunity emerges, you can snap in a new capability without having to tear apart the rest of your system.

Flexibility stars with if-then thinking. If "this" happens, then we would need to have "that option" to respond quickly. Here are a couple of brief examples to get you started:

- If a core team member quit suddenly, then we would need someone in place ready to step in temporarily until we replace them. (Solution: cross-train key roles).

- If our main supplier is experiencing delays, then we would need an alternative to fill orders and keep clients happy. (Solution: build relationships with secondary suppliers that you can turn to when you need to backfill capacity.)

- If we close all the big deals in our pipeline, then we won't be able to handle the workload next quarter. (Solution: consider looking for sources of freelance or temporary help to cover demand in the short term, or consider hiring additional staff if the increased demand is likely to be permanent.)

What other predictable disruptions can you think of that should have a plan in place? Make a list of everything that could happen in your business that would disrupt your current stability. Assign a probability to each one, then focus on possible solutions for the most likely scenarios.

What would need to be in place in your business today to allow you to roll out each of those solutions within a few days or weeks? Those are the pieces you need to build into your current structure. Structural flexibility will take different forms depending on the type of business you operate.

- **Services:** consider cross-functional team training, fractional delivery models, shorter, more focused engagements, or multiple pricing tiers for the same core service.
- **Retail:** explore ecommerce options, third-party fulfillment, or introduce pop-up concepts to test new markets.
- **Produce-based business:** consider testing on-demand production, build a more distributed supply chain, or introduce flexible packaging and bundling options.

Your goal is simple. Configure the underlying structure of your business so that you can respond quickly, recover faster, and seize new ground while others are still resetting.

Embrace Values-Aligned Leadership

The unfortunate truth is that many leaders view culture and values as aspirational rather than operational necessities. They describe an ideal they hope will attract top quality people, without ever pausing to consider what it will take to truly embody those values or how they must show up in order to cultivate it. These same leaders then wonder why they struggle to keep their people truly engaged.

Leadership hypocrisy is easily glossed over when times are good, but becomes painfully visible under pressure. How you show up under stress reveals the truth and your people quickly learn whether your culture is real or just a set of buzzwords painted on the wall. If they lose faith in your values, they will disengage long before they abandon ship. And a disengaged team is devastating to your resilience.

As Ron Tite puts it in *The Purpose of Purpose*, true leadership isn't about control, it *is taking specific actions, based on available information, to improve the lives of others*[15]. Values-aligned leadership, demonstrated through acting with integrity and consistency, is central to building a crisis-proof business. It requires you to both listen to your people and act on what they share with you.

In business as in life, your actions and the actions you tolerate from others are what will define your true culture. Take a moment to establish guidelines for how you expect the people who fill leadership roles on your team to engage with each other, with you, and with their own teams. Hold yourself accountable to those guidelines and you will find it easy to hold others accountable also. Even if your leadership has been wobbly, it's not too late to change how you show up.

When you invest in your people, treat them with respect, and cultivate shared accountability, they'll step up when it counts. They'll go the extra mile, offer solutions, and lean into the mission. And you? You become a leader who earns trust every day through quiet, steady choices that prioritize people and align with the guiding purpose of the business.

Engage in Rhythmic Strategic Planning & Realignment

A crisis-proof business is one that stays on course. That's where rhythm comes in – a repeatable, predictable system that keeps everyone focused, aligned, and accountable.

At 33Dolphins, this system is a core tool in the leadership engine of the Growth Architecture Framework. A cadence-based approach that keeps your long-term vision grounded in short-term execution, it's designed to embed a structured operating rhythm that keeps your business aligned and adaptable in real time. There are five key components to that system and each one has a role in keeping your organization on track.

Growth Clarity Blueprint

Your Growth Clarity Blueprint is the anchor around which all of your strategic efforts are built. It keeps you grounded in customer obsession and your authentic value proposition. You used it to realign your organization in Act II, and you will continue to use it as a reference point to set the context for every aspect of your strategic planning and goal setting going forward. It is the heartbeat of your growth.

The Annual Strategy Reset

This is where you define your big goals and get clear on what matters most right now. It moves the vision set out in your Blueprint into practical action and measurable interim goals by answering "Where are we going and what will it take to get there in one to three years?"

I encourage my clients to set one big goal that feels achievable yet lives on the distant horizon. That big goal sets your direction. Next decide how far you can possibly get this year. This is your one-year goal. Finally, break this goal into its component parts. What needs to happen in each quarter to make your goal a reality? Now that you have the goalposts defined, decide who will be accountable for delivering which outcomes and task them with developing the action plan and budget required to achieve them.

You may be eager to roll out your grand plan to the entire team. Take a pause first. Bring your leadership team back together for an integrity check. Is anyone sceptical that their goals can be achieved? Are you prepared to make the investment required to achieve your goal? If not, why not?

If you get a wholehearted "yes", go ahead and get the team fired up. If not, you have three options: adjust the goal to fit what's realistic within your budget, find capital investment to fund your growth, or extend the timeline and simplify the plan to remove complexity.

Be wary of planning frameworks that encourage you to set a 10-year vision. These approaches are anchored in an economic environment that no longer exists. Today's reality is that you can't possibly know what's available to you that far out. Modern economic systems experience rapid disruption that reshapes the playing field in much shorter time frames. As a small or mid-sized business owner, you have the advantage of being nimble. Don't bog yourself down in a weighty vision that's really nothing more than a pipe-dream.

David LaCombe, my friend and colleague, frames this as trying to see beyond the horizon. He considers it one of the major weaknesses in rigid business operating systems like EOS, an evaluation I agree with. The destination you're pouring your heart and soul into may not even exist in 10-years. When you focus on the horizon that you can see and recalibrate your vision annually, you will go farther with more clarity, confidently navigating the seas ahead.

Quarterly Plan-Do-Reviews

The purpose of the quarterly plan-do-review is to ensure each team knows their specific priorities and how those priorities feed into the larger business goals. In each session. you will agree on priorities for the coming quarter, review the results of your efforts in the current quarter, and agree on what you need to do to address any roadblocks or take advantage of unexpected wins and opportunities.

Come from a place of curiosity about what's changing that you need to address. What do you need to do more (or less) of? And what needs to be evaluated and possibly stopped altogether? Each team should be prepared to share:

- Did we hit our targets? If not, why?
- What needs to happen for us to meet this quarter's goals & what's in the way?
- What do we plan to stop doing? Start doing? Or do differently?
- What new opportunities are emerging?

If you have a larger team, it's generally more effective to have each leader conduct an operational level plan-do-review with their own teams, then bring the leadership team together to share the outcomes of those sessions with each other and finalize the quarterly objectives at the company level. This is also the time to discuss your quarterly metrics with your leadership team, and at your discretion with the company at large.

Monthly Metrics Reviews

Reviewing functional metrics with each team or department lets you know if they are on track to meet the quarter's goals. You will need a way to track and measure KPIs so that you can report on performance, celebrate wins, diagnose gaps, and align on necessary course corrections. If your team is large enough, have your team leads handle these meetings individually then bring them together to get you up to speed.

It's important that monthly reviews be conducted in a culture of transparency and learning, not blame. The moment people feel that admitting a challenge leads to backlash, they will stop telling the full truth and you'll lose sight of what's really going on until it's too late to fix it. Address poor performance through HR, not in this forum.

Weekly Team Check-ins

Weekly check-ins keep execution sharp. A good weekly check-in will surface performance issues and roadblocks early, providing coaching opportunities for team leaders. These meetings are where the rubber hits the road: quick, focused conversations on project progress, roadblocks, and resource needs.

Your goal is to keep the entire organization rowing in the same direction without wasting any one person's time in more meetings than is necessary. Smaller teams might meet as a group in a weekly stand-up, or you may prefer to meet with each person individually for a shorter time frame. A larger business with several departments might have team leaders conduct departmental check-ins, then bring the leadership team together to solve cross functional issues.

This rhythm embeds adaptability into your culture by consistently scanning the horizon, measuring your results, and adjusting course while there's still time to make a difference.

What Happens When You Miss The Target

You've built the plan, you're holding the meetings, and you're touching base with your team. But something is still missing. Targets aren't hit on schedule. The needle isn't moving fast enough.

I hear this a lot from leaders as they make the shift to a more proactive, crisis-ready approach. I want to hear it. Even the best laid plans experience road bumps and the strategic planning systems in the Growth Architecture Framework are designed to surface them early.

It's when leaders tell me everything is going swimmingly that I worry. If you aren't experiencing challenges, either you're playing it too safe or someone is lying. Seeing the bumps in the road means your systems are working. Now it's time to get brutally honest about the gaps that remain. Treat each challenge as a puzzle you get paid to solve and use the tools in Act II: Realign to help you solve them.

Often, expectations were set optimistically, and all that's needed is patience or minor adjustments to reflect your operational reality.

Sometimes, there is a disconnect between what the market is doing and where you believed it was heading. When this happens, test incremental adjustments to the areas that are faltering so that you are better informed when it comes time for your annual strategy reset.

Leadership behaviors are a common culprit in holding your organization back. You might want to empower your team, but find yourself micromanaging or struggling to trust the process. Or a newly hired leader might demand that everyone adapt to their preferences, oblivious to the disruption it's creating. Identifying and addressing behavioral gaps in leadership is essential if you want your systems to scale.

Whatever challenges your organization faces, I know one thing for sure. You have what it takes and you can solve whatever challenges come your way, so long as you remain connected to the community you serve and show up authentically, in alignment with the landscape you have defined for your organization.

This sounds like hard work.

Embracing a structured leadership cadence can feel overwhelming at first. This work will take patience, discipline, and support. But the shift has already started. It began the moment that you brought your team together to align around a shared strategic vision. That clarity at the top sets the tone for everything else. Give yourself permission to start where you are, not where you think you should be.

You're human and you're going to slip up. Accept it and move on. If you find you're really struggling, please don't cheat yourself in the name of fiscal responsibility. Invest in a coach or advisor who can become your guide and your sounding board. It just might save your business.

Whatever you do, don't cheat yourself of the prize when you're almost at the finish line.

Final Takeaway

The secrets to a crisis-proof business are modern-day leadership tools that empower you to face choppy waters yet still surge ahead. Your crisis-proof business model is a launchpad for your future and the work you've done to get here has already set you apart. As you continue to build your business, keep these three principles in mind:

- Even a resilient business will get rocked from time to time. You have the ability to regain your footing quickly and move forward.
- Proactive preparation is the only real safeguard. If you wait for the next crisis to unfold, you'll always be trapped in reactive mode.
- The choice to emerge stronger is up to you. Keep building, adjusting, and believing so that when the next wave hits, you'll be ready to ride it.

Will you do what it takes to create a resilient culture of committed people who are ready to adapt when times change?

HOW ALEX BECAME CRISIS-PROOF

Alex's advisor played a key role in helping him stay on track as the new training division began to take off. Together, they installed regular performance reporting, beginning with Alex's financials. They worked out how much runway he would need to survive another crisis, building a nest egg that would carry the business through without putting his home at risk. Alex also reinvested a portion of his profit back into the business to continue growing his core services.

At the same time, they held the first quarterly plan-do-review session. Alex gave his leadership team an update on the firm's financial health. Then they clearly defined what needed to happen in the coming 90 days to ensure they would reach their long-term goals. Alex also scheduled weekly check-ins with each leader. Ahead of those meetings, Alex received updated KPI reports so that they could focus their time together solving problems, not sharing data. Each leader also conducted weekly check-ins with their own team.

Alex built his own leadership muscle, learning to delegate authority and accountability without losing connection to the pulse of his business. He also began to spot challenges sooner, working with his team to resolve them quickly. As momentum started to build, Alex felt more on top of his business than he ever had and his leadership team felt empowered to contribute at a new level.

15

FROM CRISIS-PROOF TO FUTURE-READY

Your efforts to implement a leadership engine designed to navigate the next storm have delivered an added benefit. They set you on the path to becoming a more strategic CEO. And that's exactly what you need to do if your business is to graduate from crisis-proof to future-ready.

Future-ready businesses don't just weather change. They anticipate it and they capitalize on it. The systems you're about to add to your operating model are designed to plug into the foundations you have already built. Their purpose is to complete your transition from a defensive to a proactive posture that continuously innovates to remain relevant over time.

You might be wondering why we didn't just start here to begin with. It's impossible to go straight from survival mode to laser-targeted, long-term vision. Like Maslow's hierarchy of needs, your human biology is hard-wired to prevent self-actualization thinking while you're still worried about making payroll.

Maslow's Hierarchy of Needs for Business

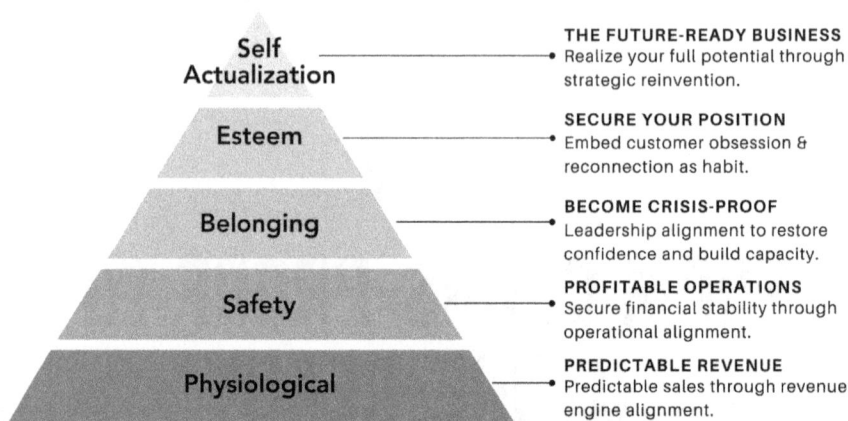

Self Actualization

THE FUTURE-READY BUSINESS
Realize your full potential through strategic reinvention.

Esteem

SECURE YOUR POSITION
Embed customer obsession & reconnection as habit.

Belonging

BECOME CRISIS-PROOF
Leadership alignment to restore confidence and build capacity.

Safety

PROFITABLE OPERATIONS
Secure financial stability through operational alignment.

Physiological

PREDICTABLE REVENUE
Predictable sales through revenue engine alignment.

For future-ready thinking to even be possible, you must first restore operational stability, reboot your revenue engine, reconnect with your most aligned customers and rebuild your own confidence by becoming crisis-proof. That work is now behind you. In this chapter, we'll explore:

- The signals that suggest a pivot may be on the horizon.
- What it takes to become a future-ready CEO
- How to use the Foresight Flywheel to prepare for, and shape, what's next.
- A modern approach to scenario planning that works for small and mid-sized businesses.

Why Now is The Perfect Time to Consider a Pivot

Even with all the work that you have done to shore up your business, the pace of technological change guarantees that you will eventually come to a place of diminishing returns. What happens when your industry is again disrupted by an outside force that no one saw coming?

Considering a strategic pivot is as simple as asking "how can we show up in a way that better meets the *likely future* needs of our customers?"

The sooner you put those wheels in motion, the more likely you'll be ready to capitalize when those future needs materialize. Becoming future-ready is how you gain the kind of foresight that builds lasting advantage.

You already have the tools you need in your toolbox. You learned them in Act I: Rethink. Sometimes grabbing an opportunity will mean shifting by only a few degrees. Others will require a total reinvention. Either way, you will have more influence over both the timing and the pace.

Recognize When It's Time To Pivot

The signals are always there, although we business owners aren't always ready to accept them. By now, the most obvious ones should sound very familiar:

- You face increasing price pressure, despite rising costs.
- It's harder to close new business, even with existing clients.
- Your pipeline is shrinking, even though you're investing in lead gen.

Sometimes the signals are less concrete. You can't quite put words to them. It just feels like you're on a speeding train, heading for a brick wall and you don't have any brakes. Worse, you're not quite sure why you feel that way. If this happens to you, pay attention. You're more in tune with your customers than you have ever been. You may be sensing the very beginning of a significant market shift.

That's what was happening to me in the story I shared with you in Customer Obsession. I had sensed the energetic shift that predicted our base of large enterprise clients was moving towards bringing our work in-house. My anxiousness preceded the concrete market signals by more than a year. Based on advice from my coaches, I chose to ignore it. As you now know, that was an almost fatal mistake. I would have been better served to focus my energy on answering *"Where is our market headed?"*

A future-ready business is one that continuously scans the environment for possible answers to that same question. They will tell you whether or not this is the time to make a significant change.

Before we dive into the tactical steps to make that happen, it's important to address two devastating enemies of the future-ready CEO, the panic pivot and the myth of the perfect plan.

Avoid the Panic Pivot

Panic pivots aren't pivots at all. They're emotional decisions masquerading as strategy. They happen when your chaos hangover is triggered. You hit a small bump in the road and taking action suddenly feels urgent. Trapped in an emotional cycle of loss aversion and action bias, you recruit your team to solve the problem and groupthink takes over.

Panic pivots arise when decisions are made in isolation, without consulting the people closest to your customer. They often involve dramatic overcorrections. And they rarely work. As you are evaluating where the market is headed, consciously check your own biases. Future-ready CEOs embody discipline and emotional intelligence. They slow down long enough to challenge their assumptions. They ask questions that invite others to challenge their conclusions.

The Myth of the Perfect Plan

Believing you can chart a foolproof path isn't just fallacy, it's perfectionism as an excuse. The perfect plan doesn't exist. There are simply too many unknowns — market dynamics, regulatory changes, technology shifts, and, frankly, human behavior.

When you catch yourself pursuing perfection over action, do a gut check. Do you have a clear, emotionally resonant vision of what your ideal future looks like? If you are clear about the destination, you already know the direction in which to move. Rather than waiting for perfection, accept that you can't possibly see farther than the horizon and trust your crisis-proof management systems to let you know when a course correction is needed.

Become a Future-Ready CEO

Let's talk about what it really means to be a future-ready leader. There is no magic. No developing psychic powers. Not even perfect predictions. And it never results from sitting in a drab room with your executive team spit-balling what the world might look like in ten years over cold coffee and a half-eaten tray of stale fruit. Being future-ready simply means becoming methodical in how you think about change.

Future-ready CEOs ask better questions, surround themselves with people who challenge assumptions, and consistently carve out time to explore what might be coming next. Combined, these habits produce strategic foresight.

Future-ready leadership teams embody these same qualities. They continuously scan the horizon for clues to what's coming, sharing their insights openly without fear of ridicule. The primary tool of the future-ready leader is the Foresight Flywheel — an underlying rhythm that boosts the impact of everything else you have already built.

The Foresight Flywheel

A future-ready planning cadence leverages the Foresight Flywheel to turn strategic foresight into action that gains momentum over time. The Foresight Flywheel is a modern riff on scenario planning. It's less crystal ball, more critical thinking, enhanced with the power of modern causal AI tools that are surprisingly accessible for even small and midsize businesses.

The Foresight Flywheel

A continuous loop of scanning for signals, mapping what could happen, and simulating strategic moves before committing.

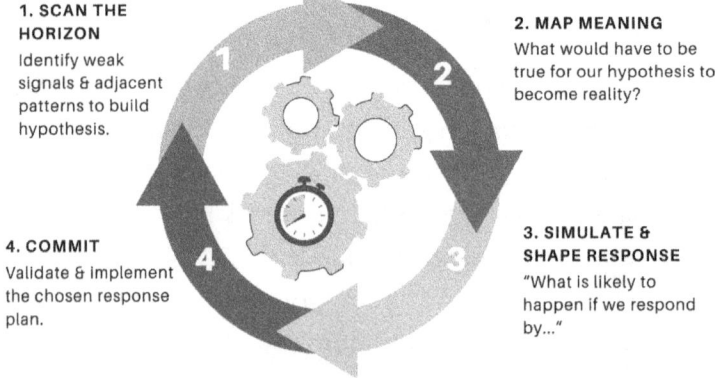

1. SCAN THE HORIZON
Identify weak signals & adjacent patterns to build hypothesis.

2. MAP MEANING
What would have to be true for our hypothesis to become reality?

4. COMMIT
Validate & implement the chosen response plan.

3. SIMULATE & SHAPE RESPONSE
"What is likely to happen if we respond by..."

The Foresight Flywheel is your system to continually scan the market for subtle shifts and early signals, then use causal thinking to map how those shifts might unfold. Finally, you will simulate small, strategic experiments that shape your next move.

By plugging the Foresight Flywheel into your planning process, you are building the muscles to engage with change earlier, more clearly, and with less emotional friction. The best part? It's not that complicated.

The Flywheel in Action

At first, it takes effort to get a flywheel turning. You have to train yourself, and then your team, to look past the day-to-day and notice what's changing. You have to get better at asking the right questions. You have to carve out space to test small, strategic moves when everything else is screaming for stability.

Once that wheel starts turning? The energy in your business moves with more ease. Positive change starts showing up earlier. You adapt faster as uncertainty becomes your advantage instead of your enemy.

Let's break down the three stages of the Flywheel and the specific tactics you will employ in each one.

Stage 1: Scan for Weak Signals

As a future-ready business, you will build the discipline of horizon scanning into your culture. By staying alert to what's shifting at the edges of your industry, customer base, or even society at large, you are more likely to spot a potential change on the horizon.

✌ Put It To Work

- **Review customer conversations regularly to spot changing language.** The people who talk to your customers every day are sitting on a goldmine. Ask them to report regularly on what customers are asking about, the language they actually use, where they're getting stuck, and what's making them hesitate. Shifts in how your customers speak are subconscious signals that provide hints about which way the winds are headed, particularly when paired with feeling words that describe new problems they're facing or familiar problems that are impacting them differently. By paying attention to how language is changing, you'll be better able to spot how their priorities are shifting.

- **Ask "What's no longer true that used to be?"** One of the simplest scans you can conduct is introduce this question regularly into team meetings. Ask it of your direct reports at the end of your monthly metrics reviews. Allocate 10 minutes at the end of each quarterly Plan-Do-Review for a discussion on this topic.

- **Use AI to summarize industry news.** Our modern society is filled with tools for synthesizing and summarizing information to keep you up-to-date with what's changing in the wider world around you. You can set up AI agents to scan major news sources and, based on your prompts, email you a daily update about what's being talked about that's relevant to your interests. Start here, then highlight signals you want to explore further.

- **Validate with research.** Once you've identified signals of interest, it's important to gather hard data to validate if what you are noticing is truly part of a bigger trend. That means research. It doesn't need to be expensive but it does need to provide you with quantitative data to support your observations.

Stage 2: Map What Would Have to Be True

This step is about identifying possible pathways that cause a fringe signal to become a tipping point. By thinking ahead to what would need to happen for the shift you've observed to become a more wide-spread change impacting your business model, you create an opportunity to recognize and react to an inflection point before it arrives. One good way to embed this into your culture is to use your quarterly leadership plan-do-review as an opportunity to review any signals your team has noticed, and decide if any are strong enough that they merit deeper exploration. Then assign the steps below to the appropriate teams, or schedule a special leadership session to address them.

ℳ Put It To Work

- **Workshop scenarios.** This begins with making a guess at what the signals you have identified mean for the future, then questioning what conditions would need to be present for that hypothesis to be a reality. There are many ways to do this. With my clients, I approach this work using the method introduced by McGrath & MacMillan in their 2005 book *Discovery-Driven Growth*,[16] and popularized by McKinsey & Company in their "What would have to be true?" format.

- **Document your hypotheses.** You may come up with multiple possible triggers that could tip a weak signal into a major trend. Most of those triggers won't be real in the moment, but may be possible in a few months or even a year. Document each pathway you workshop, including the necessary conditions you have identified, along with any assumptions or dependencies that exist. Revisit these conclusions quarterly in your leadership Plan-Do-Review sessions. Are the signals getting stronger or have they faded and the scenario is now unlikely to happen?

- **Test your conclusions using AI.** AI has birthed an entirely new category of analytics tools rooted in what's commonly known as Causal AI. These cause-and-effect mapping tools let even small teams explore "what if" scenarios using the data they already have. Modern user interfaces make the tools accessible to the average leader, no PhD in research mathematics necessary. These tools offer you an unprecedented opportunity to validate your thinking using real-world data and predictive analytics. When you integrate them into your strategic toolbox, you provide your business with an early mover advantage. As causal AI remains an emerging field of analytics, I won't include specific solutions here. However you will find references in the resource center at the front of this book.

Stage 3: Simulate and Shape the Response

This is where you convert insight into action. Shortlist the signals that are reverberating the loudest and consider what might actually happen if you act on your insights. Develop a list of possible responses your organization could take. Then develop likely scenarios using the question "what's likely to happen if we..." for each of the responses you are considering. Finally, test your conclusions using a constrained low-risk test and observe what happens. Based on the results of your test, you can either lock in your response plan or reconsider your conclusions.

ঽ৯ Put It To Work

- **Use Causal AI to Predict the Future.** The same causal AI tools that you used to validate your answers to *what would have to be true*, are invaluable in answering *what would happen if*. In this

173

situation, you ideally want a toolset that offers you access to synthetic data - computer-generated datasets that simulate real business conditions, helping you explore options and predict probable outcomes before putting real dollars at risk.

- **Run a real-world, safe-to-fail test.** Causal AI scenarios will only get you so far. They're designed to predict human behavior within varying degrees of certainty, but they still depend on you making your best guess. In a perfect world, you will validate these outcomes using real-world results. The ideal candidate for this test will be something fast and easily reversible. Your goal is low risk, limited exposure. For example, you might test a new offer with one segment or launch a beta version of a new offer and gather feedback on its impact.

By embedding the Foresight Flywheel into your rhythmic strategic planning and realignment systems, you stop reacting to the present and start shaping tomorrow. That's what being future-ready looks like.

Your Turn at the Flywheel

The best way to build a new muscle is to practice. Pick one thing that's been bothering you and, rather than push it aside, start scanning. What's changing around it? What else is connected? These are your signals.

Make a list of what would have to be true for this signal to become something bigger, and outline a small test that will help you learn without risking the whole ship. Run that test and see what happens. Were the results what you expected? What did you learn?

Key Takeaway

Future-ready CEOs don't wait for certainty or demand a perfect plan. They just find the courage to take one smarter step at a time. They gain competitive advantages by scanning the horizon to see change coming and responding without burning down what they've built. They stop waiting for the world to change around them and start changing how they operate within it.

HOW ALEX USED THE FORESIGHT FLYWHEEL

As soon as the business was stable, Alex turned his focus to the coming year. He set up an AI agent to send him a weekly update of industry news tailored to the kind of signals he was looking for. With more free time thanks to a stronger leadership team, he began attending more networking events and asking questions designed to surface where prospects were feeling stuck or uncertain. He also began chatting with his client relationship managers, to stay connected to what existing clients were sharing. At the start of each quarterly plan-do-review, Alex set the stage by asking "What is no longer true today that was true the last time we met?"

By the time the Annual Strategy Reset came around, Alex and his team had identified several signals that suggested their training programs were a differentiator that could become the gateway to larger clients. They validated their assumption ahead of the meeting, spending their time together focused on mapping what would have to be true and creating a Statement of Opportunity they could use as a starting point for both estimating potential in partnership with a causal analytics firm, and then launching a safe-to-fail market test to validate their idea before disrupting the wider operations of the organization.

By the mid-way point of year two, Alex's firm was regularly invited to bid on bigger contracts with larger manufacturing and distribution companies. And Alex? He was already scanning the market, and considering whether (and when) he could spin-off his training services as a separate company under its own brand.

16

CONCLUSION: TURN CHAOS INTO OPPORTUNITY

You now know something most business owners don't. Chaos isn't just a moment to survive, it's something you can use to your advantage so that you can start creating what's next.

Throughout this book, we've dismantled the dangerous myths that keep businesses stuck in defensive mode. You've seen how pulling back on marketing, freezing decision-making, or clinging to outdated systems might *feel* like safety, but often does more harm than good. You've also seen what works. Aligning around customer obsession as the anchor for a robust revenue engine, efficient operations, smart technology adoption, and bold, disciplined leadership.

You have the tools. You've seen the playbook. You know what survival mode looks like and you know it's not where real leaders stay. Now comes the hard part. Because knowing what to do and doing it are two very different things. So as we come to the close of this journey, here are three things I want you to remember:

1. **You don't need certainty to act.** You need clarity. And you now have a framework for finding it.

2. **Thriving in tough times is a strategy.** It requires focus, discipline, and willingness to challenge your own assumptions.

3. **Every crisis reveals both cracks and opportunities.** If you're willing to look with fresh eyes and make hard calls, you can rebuild even stronger than before.

I'll leave you with one final question: **What's the first move your future business needs you to make?** Whatever it is, do it today. Don't wait for the market to recover. Don't wait for permission. Don't wait until your competitors pull ahead. Make the move.

This is your business and the power to shape its future lies with you. Your progress depends on no one else. Seize this moment to navigate chaos and build the life and business you deserve. If you need help, whether that's with clarity, execution, or simply to find your anchor in the storm, I invite you to reach out. It would be my privilege to work with you.

Your Next Steps

Don't wait for the market to recover, start creating your future now. If you're committed to accelerating your business, I invite you to apply for a complimentary, no-strings Growth Clarity Call to help you identify your biggest growth levers and map a smarter path forward.

Book your call at 33dolphins.com/R3-GCC

BONUS MATERIALS & REFERENCES

CHAOS PATTERNS OVER THE LAST CENTURY

Here is a brief summary of each major event, including the impact it had on the economy and the survival strategies that proved most effective.

Great Depression (1929-1939): The 1929 stock market crash triggered a banking collapse, wiping out savings and sending unemployment soaring. The U.S. government's response, trade protectionism through the Smoot-Hawley Tariff Act, was devastating[17]. It is widely believed to have made the Great Depression much worse than necessary. Recovery took a decade and required massive government intervention through the New Deal[18]. A few notable brands you'll recognize, including Kellogg's[19], Proctor & Gamble[20], and Disney[21], bucked the downward trend by leaning into marketing and innovation, betting on future demand to offset short-term losses.

1970s Stagflation: The oil embargo of the early 1970s sent energy prices skyrocketing, while inflation and unemployment rose simultaneously[22]. Traditional economic tools failed to provide a quick recovery, and businesses struggled to balance increasing costs with declining demand. Those that successfully controlled operational costs and diversified their supply chains weathered the storm. During this period, McDonald's market dominance surged[23] as they reinvested in value messaging, reinforcing fast service as a differentiator while opening new locations and capitalizing on their renowned efficiency[24].

Black Monday (October 19, 1987): The stock market plunged ~22.6% in one day[25]. Although government intervention limited lasting economic damage, the crash triggered a chain reaction of events, including reduced consumer spending, a run on gold, and even bank failures. All of which had a significant impact on small and mid-sized businesses who were less well positioned to weather even a brief storm. Not to mention that this was the catalyst that saw the US dollar become the global reserve currency. Response to this period was a bellwether for some popular department store brands. Walmart opened stores and grew their supply chain infrastructure[26], taking full advantage of their price competition. Conversely, Sears invested in diversification while failing to adapt to new competitors and missing the retail reinvention moment entirely[27]. Today they maintain only a handful of stores in the United States and Puerto Rico.

Dot-Com Bubble (2000-2002): An era of rapid speculation in internet-based companies led to extreme overvaluations. When the bubble burst, venture capital dried up, and many startups collapsed. Proactive companies like Amazon[28] and Salesforce[29] focused on operational efficiency, maintaining marketing and sales investment levels despite losses. These companies emerged from the slowdown stronger. Those who focused exclusively on cost cutting, like Yahoo![30], or who accelerated marketing without managing efficiency, struggled to recover even 5 - 10 years later[31].

Global Financial Crisis (2008-2014): The housing market collapse and reckless financial practices sent shockwaves through the banking system, causing a worldwide recession[32]. Governments responded with bailouts and stimulus packages, but recovery was slow. As with the dot-com bubble, businesses that embraced digital transformation and efficiency improvements thrived in the years that followed. Lego took the opportunity to realign itself with the modern consumer, doubling down on its traditional advertising programs and leveraging experiential campaigns while leaning into innovations that expanded its product line and IP to reach new and broader markets[33]. As a result of the culture this created, Lego continues to enjoy robust growth more than 15 years later.

COVID-19 Recession (2020-Present): A global pandemic disrupted nearly every industry, with lockdowns and supply chain failures forcing rapid business adaptations[34]. Those who quickly transitioned to digital operations, remote work, and e-commerce gained an early competitive advantage. Nike rapidly accelerated direct-to-consumer and digital adoption, while expanding brand marketing and consumer engagement. This strategy yielded 75% ecommerce growth year - over - year as Nike emerged from the pandemic a solid category leader[35]. Meanwhile Under Armour pulled back on marketing spend, closed stores, delayed the launch of e-commerce and sold its connected fitness app (MyFitnessPal). Sales dropped 23%, requiring the company to rebuild and restructure operations. As of April 2025, the company had not yet been restored to its pre-COVID strength[36].

NOTES

Act I: Rethink

1 Jamais Cascio, "Facing the Age of Chaos," *Medium*, April 18, 2020, https://medium.com/@cascio/facing-the-age-of-chaos-bdc63ac9f3c5.

2 Bennis, Warren, and Burt Nanus. *Leaders: Strategies for Taking Charge*. New York: Harper & Row, 1985.

3 U.S. Department of State, Office of the Historian, "Protectionism in the Interwar Period," *Milestones in the History of U.S. Foreign Relations: 1921–1936*, accessed September 16, 2025, https://history.state.gov/milestones/1921-1936/protectionism.

4 Ranjay Gulati, Nitin Nohria, and Franz Wohlgezogen, "Roaring Out of Recession," *Harvard Business Review* (March 2010), https://hbr.org/2010/03/roaring-out-of-recession.

5 Susana Velez-Castrillón and Cory Angert, "How Sony Got Its Groove Back," *Journal of the International Academy for Case Studies* 21, no. 7 (2015): 144–154.

6 Preston Fore, "Apple Cofounder Steve Jobs Dealt with the 2008 Financial Crisis by Investing His Way Through the Downturn, Instead of Slashing Jobs and Budgets — 2 Years Later the Iconic iPad Was Launched," *Fortune*, April 10, 2025, https://fortune.com/2025/04/10/apple-cofounder-steve-jobs-investing-through-economic-crash-2008-recession-iphone-ipad-sales/.

7 Rolf Dobelli, *The Art of Thinking Clearly* (New York: Harper, 2014).

8 Carolyn Stern, *The Emotionally Strong Leader: An Inside-Out Journey to Transformational Leadership* (Vancouver: Figure 1 Publishing, 2022).

9 Shopify Inc. 2021 Annual Report. (Ottawa: Shopify Inc., 2022) https://shopifyinvestors.com/financial-reports.

10 Simon Little, "Coronavirus: B.C. Hotel Chain Finds Way to Help Healthcare Workers Who Want to Self-Isolate," *Global News*, March 23, 2020, https://globalnews.ca/news/6760441/coronavirus-b-c-hotel-

chain-finds-way-to-help-healthcare-workers-who-want-to-self-isolate/.

11 Jane McGonigal, I*maginable: How to See the Future Coming and Feel Ready for Anything — Even Things That Seem Impossible Today,* 1st ed. (New York: Spiegel & Grau, 2022).

12 WatchMyCompetitor. *6 Reasons Why Companies Decline and Lessons to Protect Your Market Share.* London: WatchMyCompetitor, September 20, 2023. https://www.watchmycompetitor.com/resources/6-reasons-why-companies-decline/

Act II: Realign

13 Luís Cabral and David Backus, Betamax and VHS *(Firms and Markets mini-case)* (New York: NYU Stern School of Business, 2002), https://pages.stern.nyu.edu/lcabral/teaching/betamax.pdf.

14 Koch, M., & Menkhoff, L. (2024, January). The non-linear impact of risk tolerance on entrepreneurial profit and business survival (DIW Discussion Paper No. 2067). Deutsches Institut für Wirtschaftsforschung (DIW Berlin). https://www.diw.de/documents/publikationen/73/diw_01.c.889271.de/dp2067.pdf

Act III: Reinvent

15 Ron Tite, *The Purpose of Purpose*: Why Your Business Is Nothing Without It (Vancouver: Page Two Books, 2022).

16 Rita Gunther McGrath and Ian C. MacMillan, Discovery-Driven Growth: *A Breakthrough Process to Reduce Risk and Seize Opportunity (*Boston: Harvard Business Press, 2009).

17 U.S. Department of State, Office of the Historian, "Protectionism in the Interwar Period," *Milestones in the History of U.S. Foreign Relations:* 1921–1936, accessed September 16, 2025, https://history.state.gov/milestones/1921-1936/protectionism.

18 U.S. Department of State, Office of the Historian, "New Deal Trade Policy: The Export-Import Bank & the Reciprocal Trade Agreements Act, 1934," *Milestones in the History of U.S. Foreign Relations:* 1921–1936, accessed

September 16, 2025, https://history.state.gov/milestones/1921-1936/export-import-bank.

19 Lauren Alex O'Hagan, "A Breakfast Revolution for Mothers?: Introducing Kellogg's Corn Flakes to the Swedish Market, 1929-1939," *History of Retailing and Consumption* 10, no. 2 (2024): 133-167, https://doi.org/10.1080/2373518X.2024.2372547.

20 WARC. "P&G's Playbook for the Recession." *WARC*, April 7, 2020. https://www.warc.com/newsandopinion/news/pgs-playbook-for-the-recession/en-gb/43522.

21 "How Mickey Got Disney Through the Great Depression," *CBC Radio: Under the Influence,* May 23, 2016, https://www.cbc.ca/radio/undertheinfluence/how-mickey-got-disney-through-the-great-depression-1.3462981.

22 Blinder, Alan S., and Jeremy B. Rudd. "The Supply-Shock Explanation of the Great Stagflation Revisited." *In The Great Inflation: Causes and Consequences*, edited by Robert E. Hall and David E. Weinstein, 123–172. NBER, 2010.

23 George Ritzer, *The McDonaldization of Society* (Thousand Oaks, CA: SAGE, 2013).

24 "McDonald's History Listing." *McDepk.com* (archival PDF on Yumpu), February 20, 2013. https://www.yumpu.com/en/document/view/10146742/mcdonalds-history-listing-mcdepkcomf.

25 International Banker, "Black Monday (1987)," *International Banker,* September 29, 2021, https://internationalbanker.com/history-of-financial-crises/black-monday-1987/.

26 Charles Fishman, *The Wal-Mart Effect* (New York: Penguin, 2006).

27 Boris Emmet and John E. Jeuck, *Catalogues and Counters: A History of Sears, Roebuck and Company* (Chicago: University of Chicago Press, 1990).

28 Eud Foundation Team. 2024. "How Successful Companies Overcome Times of Crisis: 3 Case Studies to Inspire You." *Eud International Foundation,* January 18, 2024. https://www.eudfoundation.info/post/how-successful-companies-overcome-times-of-crisis-3-case-studies-to-inspire-you.

29 Salesforce, "The History of Salesforce," *Salesforce Newsroom*, accessed September 16, 2025, https://www.salesforce.com/news/stories/the-history-of-salesforce/.

30 Wikipedia contributors, "History of Yahoo!" *Wikipedia*, last modified September 13, 2025, https://en.wikipedia.org/wiki/History_of_Yahoo.

31 Goldman Sachs, "The Late 1990s Dot-Com Bubble Implodes in 2000," Goldman Sachs: Our Firm—History, accessed September 16, 2025, https://www.goldmansachs.com/our-firm/history/moments/2000-dot-com-bubble.

32 Reserve Bank of Australia, "The Global Financial Crisis," *Explainers: Education Resources,* Reserve Bank of Australia, accessed September 16, 2025, https://www.rba.gov.au/education/resources/explainers/the-global-financial-crisis.html.

33 John Stoll, "Lego Builds Market Share as Ever-Popular Toy Bricks Defy Demand Drop," Wall Street Journal, March 7, 2024, https://www.wsj.com/business/retail/lego-builds-market-share-as-ever-popular-toy-bricks-defy-demand-drop-31af4249

34 Knut Alicke, Ed Barriball, and Vera Trautwein, "How COVID-19 Is Reshaping Supply Chains," *McKinsey & Company*, November 23, 2021, https://www.mckinsey.com/capabilities/operations/our-insights/how-covid-19-is-reshaping-supply-chains.

35 Renaldi, Mike. "The COVID-19 Pandemic Accelerates Nike's Ecommerce Focus." Vaimo, August 23, 2022. Accessed October 14, 2025. https://www.vaimo.com/blog/covid-accelerates-nike-ecommerce-focus/.

36 Anuja Bharat Mistry, "Under Armour Gets a Lift from CEO Plank's Full Price Focus, North America Recovery," *Reuters*, February 6, 2025, https://www.reuters.com/business/retail-consumer/under-armour-lifts-annual-profit-forecast-2025-02-06/.

ACKNOWLEDGEMENTS

Writing this book has been a journey shaped not just by research and reflection, but by the people who've walked alongside, challenged me, and made this work possible.

To the many bold, driven business leaders I've had the privilege to call my clients, you've been my greatest teachers. Your willingness to take risks, push through uncertainty, and pursue growth with tenacity and heart has not only informed the models in this book, but shaped the way I see the world. While there are too many of you to name individually, please know this: I carry the lessons from our work together with me always.

To my husband, thank you for walking beside me through every twist and turn of this entrepreneurial journey. Your unwavering belief gave me courage (and maybe just enough insanity) to leap. You have never once asked me to shrink. For that alone, I owe you more than words can express.

To my daughter Viktoria, your encouragement, your patience, and your confidence in me pushed this project from pipe-dream to the finish line. I'm deeply grateful for your quiet strength, keen mind, and unwavering support, especially in the final stretch.

To my son Collin, whose common sense and razor-sharp wit keep me grounded no matter what kind of chaos I'm navigating, you remind me daily to not take myself (or life) too seriously. That's a gift I treasure.

To the many generous experts I'm lucky to call colleagues and friends, thank you for lending your insights, your time, and your honesty. People like Mark Stouse, David LaCombe, Achim Klor, Cathy Kuzel, and David Newman asked questions and shared insights that challenged my thinking, expanded my perspective, and helped shape this work in meaningful ways.

Thank you all, truly

ABOUT THE AUTHOR

Paula Skaper is a Canadian business strategist, speaker, and author specializing in growth strategy, digital adoption, and AI integration for expertise-driven firms. Over three decades as an entrepreneur and advisor, she has guided organizations through recessions, globalization, and technological disruption with clarity and confidence.

As CEO of 33Dolphins, Paula helps leaders rethink assumptions, realign strategies, and reinvent their businesses for future-ready growth. Her work draws on deep experience in strategic planning, marketing, and organizational design, with a pragmatic, human-centered approach to AI adoption.

Paula is also a keynote speaker and workshop facilitator, known for her candid insights and ability to make complex ideas actionable. She lives in Vancouver, Canada , where she balances her professional work with writing, travel, and time with family.

YOUR NEXT STEPS

Don't wait for the market to recover. Start creating your future now.

If *RETHINK REALIGN REINVENT* lit a fire in your belly, don't stop here. You've seen what works. Now it's time to build it into your business.

- Download the free strategy tools and growth checklists at **33dolphins.com/R3-book** to start taking action where it matters most.
- Follow me on LinkedIn for more content: **linkedin.com/in/ paulaskaper**
- If you're committed to accelerating your business, apply for a complimentary **Growth Clarity Call**. It's a tight, focused session to help you identify your biggest growth levers and map a smarter path forward.

Book your call at 33dolphins.com/R3-GCC

www.ingramcontent.com/pod-product-compliance
Lightning Source LLC
Chambersburg PA
CBHW031851200326
41597CB00012B/364